VIOLENCE

OPPOSING VIEWPOINTS®

Other Books of Related Interest

VIOLENCE

OPPOSING VIEWPOINTS®

Laura K. Egendorf, *Book Editor*

Bonnie Szumski, *Editorial Director*
Scott Barbour, *Managing Editor*

OPPOSING
VIEWPOINTS®
SERIES NEW ENGLAND INSTITUTE
OF TECHNOLOGY
LEARNING RESOURCES CENTER
Greenhaven Press, Inc., San Diego, California

101

Cover photo: Photodisc

Library of Congress Cataloging-in-Publication Data

Violence : opposing viewpoints / Laura K. Egendorf, book editor.
  p. cm. — (Opposing viewpoints series)
  Includes bibliographical references and index.
  ISBN 0-7377-0660-0 (hardcover : alk. paper) —
ISBN 0-7377-0659-7 (pbk. : alk. paper)
  1. Violence—United States. I. Egendorf, Laura K., 1973–
II. Opposing viewpoints series (Unnumbered)

HN90.V5 V5494 2001
303.6'9073—dc21
                                                              00-050319
                                                                   CIP

Greenhaven Press, Inc., P.O. Box 289009
San Diego, CA 92198-9009

"Congress shall make no law...abridging the freedom of speech, or of the press."

First Amendment to the U.S. Constitution

The basic foundation of our democracy is the First Amendment guarantee of freedom of expression. The Opposing Viewpoints Series is dedicated to the concept of this basic freedom and the idea that it is more important to practice it than to enshrine it.

Contents

Why Consider Opposing Viewpoints?

"The only way in which a human being can make some approach to knowing the whole of a subject is by hearing what can be said about it by persons of every variety of opinion and studying all modes in which it can be looked at by every character of mind. No wise man ever acquired his wisdom in any mode but this."

John Stuart Mill

In our media-intensive culture it is not difficult to find differing opinions. Thousands of newspapers and magazines and dozens of radio and television talk shows resound with differing points of view. The difficulty lies in deciding which opinion to agree with and which "experts" seem the most credible. The more inundated we become with differing opinions and claims, the more essential it is to hone critical reading and thinking skills to evaluate these ideas. Opposing Viewpoints books address this problem directly by presenting stimulating debates that can be used to enhance and teach these skills. The varied opinions contained in each book examine many different aspects of a single issue. While examining these conveniently edited opposing views, readers can develop critical thinking skills such as the ability to compare and contrast authors' credibility, facts, argumentation styles, use of persuasive techniques, and other stylistic tools. In short, the Opposing Viewpoints Series is an ideal way to attain the higher-level thinking and reading skills s⁄ essential in a culture of diverse and contradictory opinio⁄

In addition to providing a tool for critical thinki⁄
posing Viewpoints books challenge readers to qu⁄
own strongly held opinions and assumptions⁄
form their opinions on the basis of upbri⁄
sure, and personal, cultural, or professio⁄
carefully balanced opposing views, re⁄
front new ideas as well as the opi⁄
they disagree. This is not to s⁄

one who reads opposing views will—or should—change his or her opinion. Instead, the series enhances readers' understanding of their own views by encouraging confrontation with opposing ideas. Careful examination of others' views can lead to the readers' understanding of the logical inconsistencies in their own opinions, perspective on why they hold an opinion, and the consideration of the possibility that their opinion requires further evaluation.

Evaluating Other Opinions

To ensure that this type of examination occurs, Opposing Viewpoints books present all types of opinions. Prominent spokespeople on different sides of each issue as well as well-known professionals from many disciplines challenge the reader. An additional goal of the series is to provide a forum for other, less known, or even unpopular viewpoints. The opinion of an ordinary person who has had to make the decision to cut off life support from a terminally ill relative, for example, may be just as valuable and provide just as much insight as a medical ethicist's professional opinion. The editors have two additional purposes in including these less known views. One, the editors encourage readers to respect others' opinions—even when not enhanced by professional credibility. It is only by reading or listening to and objectively evaluating others' ideas that one can determine whether they are worthy of consideration. Two, the inclusion of such viewpoints encourages the important critical thinking skill of objectively evaluating an author's credentials and bias. This evaluation will illuminate an author's reasons for taking a particular stance on an issue and will aid in readers' evaluation of the author's ideas.

It is our hope that these books will give readers a deeper ¹derstanding of the issues debated and an appreciation of ᵐplexity of even seemingly simple issues when good ᵗest people disagree. This awareness is particularly ᵗ in a democratic society such as ours in which ᵍᵃʳᵗ into public debate to determine the common carewith whom one disagrees should not be re- ᵉˢ but rather as people whose views deserve ᵗ and may shed light on one's own.

Thomas Jefferson once said that "difference of opinion leads to inquiry, and inquiry to truth." Jefferson, a broadly educated man, argued that "if a nation expects to be ignorant and free . . . it expects what never was and never will be." As individuals and as a nation, it is imperative that we consider the opinions of others and examine them with skill and discernment. The Opposing Viewpoints Series is intended to help readers achieve this goal.

Greenhaven Press anthologies primarily consist of previously published material taken from a variety of sources, including periodicals, books, scholarly journals, newspapers, government documents, and position papers from private and public organizations. These original sources are often edited for length and to ensure their accessibility for a young adult audience. The anthology editors also change the original titles of these works in order to clearly present the main thesis of each viewpoint and to explicitly indicate the opinion presented in the viewpoint. These alterations are made in consideration of both the reading and comprehension levels of a young adult audience. Every effort is made to ensure that Greenhaven Press accurately reflects the original intent of the authors included in this anthology.

Introduction

"A vast system of communications technology . . . has led to the creation of a culture of violence of unprecedented dimensions, much of it directed toward or available to children."

—journalist and professor Myriam Miedzian

"Violence is as American as cherry pie."

—former Black Panther H. Rap Brown

Statistics provided by the Bureau of Justice indicate that the rate of violent crime in the United States has fallen. In 1998, 2,776,800 violent crimes were reported, compared to the 4,191,000 incidents from just five years earlier. Yet, despite the apparent decline, violence remains a concern for much of America.

While violent crime is at a twenty-five-year low, the rate is still much higher than it was in the mid–twentieth century. According to the FBI's Unified Crime Reports, the rate of violent crime nearly quadrupled between 1960 and 1997. In 1960, the rate was 160 violent crimes per 100,000 persons. Thirty-seven years later, the rate had jumped to 611 violent crimes per 100,000 persons. Among the violent crimes that occurred in the late 1990s was a rash of school shootings, culminating in the massacre at Littleton High School in Colorado in April 1999.

Many commentators charged that the rise in youth violence was due to the influence of violent movies, video games, television programs, and song lyrics. Columnist John Leo maintains that in earlier generations, violence was depicted as a last resort in movies, and not something in which the films' heroes took pleasure. In present-day society, some observers argue, violence in the media is more prevalent and frequently glorified. Robert Stacy McCain writes in *Insight* magazine: "When children watch graphic violence in movies and TV shows and also play realistic, violent video games, it breaks down their natural resistance to killing." In December 1995, epidemiologist Brandon S.

Centerwall told *Newsweek* that without television there would be 10,000 fewer murders per year.

However, popular culture is not the only aspect of American society that has been targeted for inciting violence. Some analysts assert that the public school system is to blame. Psychologist Michael Hurd maintains that students in public schools are not taught the difference between right and wrong and are therefore more likely to commit crimes without considering their actions. He explains: "It's much easier for kids to rationalize the doing of wrong—especially on the grotesque scale we saw in Littleton, Colorado—when they are taught that there really is no such thing as right or wrong in the first place." Other commentators link the rise in violence to the concurrent growth in single-parent families. In her contribution to the book *Ending the Cycle of Violence*, Myriam Miedzian, a journalist and professor of philosophy, writes that the highest rates of violence in American society are found among males who were raised by single mothers.

Those who claim that violence in America is not the result of three decades of violent programming dispute these views. Conservative writer David Horowitz acknowledges that television violence can negatively affect youths who grow up in abusive families but contends that its effect is otherwise overstated. He writes in *American Enterprise*: "Exactly the same television is watched in South Central Los Angeles and Beverly Hills; in Detroit, Michigan and Windsor, Canada." In a commentary in *USA Today* magazine, Joe Saltzman also reiterates the argument that exposure to violence in the media does not automatically lead to violent crime, because school shootings are a rare occurrence. "Logic dictates that, if movies, television, video games, and the Internet are responsible for this kind of behavior, then why is this event so unusual? If these media so corrupt the minds and hearts and souls of America's young people, then why doesn't this kind of activity happen every day?"

Another argument exists as well. Many scholars have contended that violence is not the result of popular culture, but is instead an inherent part of American society that is unaffected by current fads or values. David T. Courtwright, the author of *Violent Land: Single Men and Social Disorder From the Frontier to the Inner City*, explains it succinctly: "Violence is the primal problem of American history, the dark reverse of its coin of freedom and abundance." In an article in *American Heritage* that was adapted from his book, Courtwright details the pattern of violence throughout American history. He notes that violence has always been most prevalent among people—particularly young men—in their teens or twenties, regardless of time or place. In addition, while the breakdown of the family is often seen as a more recent cause of violence, Courtwright observes that it has long led to crime. He writes: "Across times and cultures, children who are abandoned or illegitimate or who lack a parent . . . are statistically more prone to delinquency, truancy, dropout, unemployment, illness, injury, drug abuse, theft, and violent crime. The worst effects are most apparent in adolescent boys." *Seattle Times* columnist Jerry Large wrote during the trial of Timothy McVeigh, who was convicted for his role in the Oklahoma City bombing, that America was founded on violence—it was through war and other violent acts that the Pilgrims and settlers wrested land from Native Americans and Mexico. As Large puts it: "We owe a lot of our success to being good at using violence efficiently."

Whether or not violence in America is a new problem or one that has been a concern for more than two centuries, it is an issue that continues to garner considerable attention. In *Violence: Opposing Viewpoints*, the state of violence is debated in the following chapters: Is Violence a Serious Problem? What Are the Causes of Violence? What Factors Lead to Youth Violence? How Can Society Respond to Violence? In those chapters, the authors consider the relationship between violence and American society.

CHAPTER 1

Is Violence a Serious Problem?

Chapter Preface

Media attention is often focused on school violence, such as the April 1999 shooting in Littleton, Colorado, that led to the deaths of fourteen students, including the two gunmen, and one teacher. Just as school can sometimes prove to be a violent place for adolescents, adults often find the workplace unsafe. According to the National Institute for Occupational Safety and Health, approximately one million employees are victims of nonfatal workplace assaults every year and another one thousand employees are murdered while at work. Some of these fatalities include police officers shot while on duty or taxicab drivers killed by a passenger. In many cases, however, the assailant is a current or former coworker.

One of the first incidents of workplace violence to garner national attention occurred in Edmond, Oklahoma. On August 20, 1986, substitute letter carrier Patrick Sherrill murdered fourteen fellow employees at the Edmond post office before committing suicide. Fourteen years later, the problem of workplace violence has not disappeared. For example, on May 24, 2000, John Taylor and his friend Craig Godineaux shot seven workers, five fatally, at a Wendy's restaurant in Flushing, Queens, where Taylor had been briefly employed.

Those who perpetrate workplace violence do so for a variety of reasons. Some, for example, suffer from psychological problems. In his book, *New Arenas for Violence: Homicide in the American Workplace*, Michael D. Kelleher notes the traits that some homicidal workers possess: "Risk [of homicide] is . . . high when an individual has a history of violence . . . or suffers from an antisocial personality disorder." Surviving co-workers described Sherrill as often being angry and depressed and avoiding workplace socialization. Other violent employees are motivated by criminal impulses. Prior to his arrest for the Wendy's massacre, Taylor had been linked to a series of armed robberies at fast-food restaurants and had left his job at Wendy's under suspicion of theft.

The prevalence of violence, whether at work, school, home, or elsewhere, is a topic that has sparked considerable debate. In the following chapter, the authors consider whether violence is a serious problem.

"Criminologists . . . warn of the 'superpredators,' a class of criminal hard-wired and programmed for violence."

Violent Crime Is Getting Worse

Kenneth Lloyd Billingsley

Violent crime is worsening in the United States, argues Kenneth Lloyd Billingsley in the following viewpoint. He maintains that the rise in violence is due to the fact that criminals are younger and more impulsive than they were in the past. According to Billingsley, the rate of violent crime is likely to continue its increase, regardless of how much money the government spends to reduce crime, because there will always be violent people. Billingsley is the editorial director of the Pacific Research Institute in San Francisco, an organization that promotes the principles of personal responsibility and individual freedom.

As you read, consider the following questions:
1. According to a book cited by the author, how does the violent crime rate in the United States compare to that of Europe?
2. In Billingsley's view, how is this new breed of killer similar to kamikaze pilots?
3. According to Stanton Samenow, as cited by Billingsley, why are theories that blame society for crime incorrect?

Excerpted from Kenneth Lloyd Billingsley, "Natural Born Killers," *Heterodoxy*, March 1997. Reprinted with permission from *Heterodoxy*.

In *Crime and the Sacking of America: The Roots of Chaos*, published [in 1995], Andrew Payton Thomas notes that violent crime is four to nine times more common in the United States than in Europe. American rates of rape and robbery are seven and four times greater, respectively, than European rates. And some crime statistics make the Third World seem safe by comparison. According to Thomas, a graduate of Harvard Law School and now Arizona's assistant attorney general, the American rate for robbery is over six times the Philippines' rate, twenty times Thailand's and five hundred times Egypt's.

The Murder Rate Is Rising

In Washington, D.C., which should be the nation's showcase, the murder rate nearly doubled from 1987 to 1990, when the District was averaging two homicides a day. Washingtonians were more likely to be killed by their own countrymen, than were citizens of war-torn El Salvador, Lebanon, or Northern Ireland likely to be killed by theirs. Washington may be a largely black city, but for Thomas, a former legal assistant to the Boston NAACP, violent crime is not a black problem, no more than it is for sociologist Glenn Loury, who says it is "sin, not skin." And the numbers bear them out. The crime rate among white juveniles is now growing twice as fast as the black juvenile crime rate. Nor is this just one of those statistical blips on the screen: between 1965 and 1991, the violent crime rate among white Americans rose nearly 250 percent.

From 1990–1994, 90,000 Americans were murdered. Residents of Los Angeles are more likely to die from a bullet than a traffic accident. A resident of a large American city, today, is more likely to be a victim of homicide than the average U.S. soldier in World War II. Chicago first collected statistics for gang-related homicides in 1964, when there were ten. By 1994, it was 240, "one every business day" says Nick Howe of the Illinois Department of Corrections.

Responding to Clinton, Princeton scholar John DiIulio, *(Body Count)*, notes the actual number of serious violent crimes topped 4 million in 1992. Security measures and gated communities were on the increase, DiIulio noted, but had not translated into a drop in crime. [In August 1998], Bob Dole was cheered for citing the cause of crime as "criminals," but criminologists and prison reformers bring more definition to his laconic remark. They warn of the "superpredators," a class of criminal hard-wired and programmed for violence, like Arnold Schwarzenegger's robotic "terminator."

A New Generation of Criminals

"As high as America's body count is today, a rising tide of youth crime and violence is about to lift it even higher," says DiIulio. "A new generation of street criminals is upon us—the youngest, biggest, and baddest generation any society has ever known." This generation, he says, comprises "radically impulsive, brutally remorseless youngsters, including ever more preteenage boys, who murder, assault, rape, rob, burglarize, deal deadly drugs, join gun-toting gangs and create serious communal disorders." They will commit the most heinous acts for trivial reasons, such as a perception of "disrespect." Nothing matters to them but sex, drugs and money, and as long as their youthful energies hold out they do what comes "naturally." They are "radically present-oriented, and radically self-regarding. They lack empathic impulses; they kill or maim or get involved in other forms of serious crime without much consideration of future penalties or risk to themselves or others. The stigma of arrest means nothing to them."

Likewise, the fear of death. Like kamikaze pilots, or the Ayatollah's martyrdom-seeking human bombs, this new breed of killer does not fear being killed, but rather expects it. Theirs is the creed of John, the teenage murderer in *River's Edge*, who strangled a girl so he could have "total control over her," and later explained, "I have this philosophy, you do shit then you die."

As DiIulio, and his co-authors William Bennett and John Walters note in *Body Count*, while the rate of murders by adults has declined more than 25 percent since 1985, the homicide rate among 18- to 24-year-olds increased by 61 percent and the rate of homicide committed by teenagers 14–17 more than doubled. Males 14–24 are now about 8 percent of population but represent 27 percent of all homicide victims and 48 percent of all murderers. Between 1985 and 1992, the rate at which males 14–17 committed murder increased by about 50 percent for whites and more than 300 percent for blacks.

"I laugh at the news about crime going down," says Sgt. Wes McBride of the Los Angeles County Sheriff's Department, a national authority on gangs. "There are violent little monsters out there and we are raising a whole generation of monsters. A priest said don't demonize them. I say that's what they are." McBride says that the up-and-comers often strike fear into the hearts of even older gang members. "The older guys say 'we can't even go out and wash our cars.'" And if the young toughs decide to shoot it up "they don't ask anybody."

An Explosion of Juvenile Crime

James Q. Wilson, the nation's premier criminologist, describes the young felons of today as "feral pre-social beings," and estimates that by the year 2000 there will be one million more people in the 14–17 bracket, which now counts 7.5 million boys. Some 6 percent of these boys, warns Wilson, "will become high-rate, repeat offenders—thirty thousand more young muggers, killers and thieves than we have now. Get ready."

Andrew Thomas sees America being sacked by "home-grown barbarians." He cites "a terrifying social phenomenon in the United States—a generation of 'stone killers,' generally young men, emerging across the country. They are criminals apparently wholly lacking in conscience, for whom murder carries no more remorse than grocery shopping. These young men, whose ranks are growing rapidly in number and notoriety, have stained the nation's sidewalks and focused our attention on crime like nothing in our history.". . .

In 1965, according to FBI statistics, more than 90 percent of murders resulted in a suspect's arrest. At present, more than one third of all murderers elude apprehension. As John Di-Iulio and his collaborators note in *Body Count*, despite a 91 percent increase in the rate of minors charged with crime over the last decade, the average sentence for homicide is 149 months, with the average time served coming a paltry 43 months, less than 48 percent of the sentence. Kidnappers serve 50 percent of their sentence, robbers 46 percent and those who commit assault 48 percent. Further, 13 percent of minors charged with violent crimes have them dismissed, 13 percent are sent to adult court, 16 percent to juvenile detention, and 28 percent to "other" supposed solutions such as probation and community service. But with recidivism rates in the United States as high as 75 percent—55 percent of Chino inmates repeat—those who do a stretch will soon be back.

An Alarming Report

Rosy assessments of the nation's declining crime rate wrongly focus on short-term drops from crime peaks early in the decade and ignore the overall rise of violence since the 1960s, according to a report.

The 30-year update of a landmark study by the National Commission on the Causes and Prevention of Violence found that violent crime in major cities reported to the FBI has risen by 40 percent since 1969.

The new study is intended as a counterpoint to the drumbeat of optimistic reports describing the current drop in crime, and it offers a sober reminder that the United States still suffers from a historically high level of violence.

David A. Vise and Lorraine Adams, *Washington Post National Weekly Edition*, December 13, 1999.

DiIulio, a Democrat, warns of those now growing up surrounded by "deviant, delinquent, criminal adults, in fatherless, godless and jobless settings." That kind of "criminogenic" environment is the breeding ground for the new breed of criminal. He is not surprised that the rate of homicide by youths under 17 tripled between 1984 and 1994, which could boost the total of juvenile murders 25 percent by 2005. This at a time when the number of 15–19-year-olds of all races is expected to rise 23 percent before 2005.

Explaining Violence

"The viciousness and the increasing frequency of the predators on the national scene," writes Andrew Thomas, "have led Americans to wonder what possibly could have brought about such mindless brutality. The answer requires tracing consequences back to their original ideas."

"Since the late 19th century there has been a prevalent opinion that society is more to blame for crime than the criminal," writes psychiatrist Stanton Samenow in *Inside the Criminal Mind*, grappling with a notion that is part of the genetic structure of the Left. More recently, "sociologists assert that the inner-city youngster responds with rage to a society that has excluded him from the mainstream and made the American dream beyond his reach. Some contend that crime is a normal and adaptive response to growing up in the soul-searing conditions of places like Watts and the South Bronx." The only trouble with these social theories, Samenow found, was that they did not square with reality.

It was "unwarranted and racist," Samenow Said, to assume that because a person is poor or a minority he is inadequate to cope with his environment and therefore could not become a criminal. He found that violent criminals came from all strata of society, not just poor areas, that they had rejected their parents, not the other way around, and that they were not forced into a life of crime and violence but rather chose it. Criminals know right from wrong and "believe that whatever they want to do at any given time is right for them. Their crimes require logic and self-control." He concluded that "crime resides within the minds of human beings and is not caused by social conditions." Further, "there are people who will be exploitative, larcenous, and violent no matter what the laws are."

And no matter, one should add, how much the government spends. The rise in crime has accompanied a five-fold increase in social spending since the 1960s. Lack of money is not the problem. Echoing Bob Dole, Samenow says that criminals themselves are the problem. Criminals are "at heart anti-work" and believe that taking a job means "to sell your soul, to be a slave." The criminal "believes that he is entitled to whatever he desires. . . . Many of the criminal's fantasies range beyond what is feasible, but once he comes up with an idea that seems plausible, he nourishes it until he is positive that he can enact it without a hitch. . . . Wherever the criminal is . . . he visualizes people and property as opportunities for conquest." Criminals "crave power for its own sake, and they will do virtually anything to acquire it. Insatiable in their thirst for power and unprincipled in their exercise of it, they care very little whom they injure or destroy."

"Crime is down. And not only is it down; it's way down."

Violent Crime Is Decreasing

Matthew Gore

In the following viewpoint, Matthew Gore argues that the rate of violent crime in the United States is decreasing. Gore asserts that there have several reasons why crime is becoming less of a problem, including changing demographics and anti-crime legislation. However, he notes that this decline is not widely known because it is not reported in the media, which tends to sensationalize crime. Gore is a features writer and associate editor for the *Prison Mirror*.

As you read, consider the following questions:
1. According to statistics cited by the author, by how much did the rate of violent crime decrease between 1993 and 1998?
2. According to Gore, what is one of the likeliest reasons for the declining crime rate?
3. What might happen if American society does not take the time to find out why crime exists, in Gore's opinion?

Reprinted from Matthew Gore, "The Falling Crime Rate," *The Prison Mirror*, October 1999. Reprinted with permission from the author.

It's no longer an anomaly. It has been sustained far too long now to be just a short-term blip. What it's become, folks, is a bona fide trend, and the trend continues. When people talk about trends and crime, they normally talk with fatalistic visions of the future about an out of control crime rate: the need for high-security homes, no strolls after dusk, and the real possibility that anyone at anytime can suddenly become a crime statistic. Why then should we be at all surprised that the television and print news media don't know how to talk about this new, unexpected trend in the crime rate?

A Trend That Has Been Ignored

Yes, crime is down. And not only is it down; it's way down. The crime rate has been falling relatively fast for several years. But few of us would know it. This is one trend that apparently has been deemed unworthy of our attention. The stock market is on an eight-year upward trend. This we know. The economy's humming right along on a trend that most Americans are benefiting from in sonic form or fashion. And the trend in the '90s is to have an SUV. But unless reading a newspaper is as much a part of your daily routine as showering, you are not likely to know anything about this trend: that your chances of falling victim to crime are hardly worth worrying about. But as much as everyone is concerned about crime, barely a word is said of this new trend. Perhaps fears that acknowledging the declining crime rate as a trend will quickly end it causes our trepidation over discussing the subject. Whatever the reason for the silence, it needs to end.

Trends are exactly what they are: sustained periods of growth or decline that have a beginning and an ending. Trends do indeed end, maybe not now but undoubtedly at some point. This trend too will end—and almost certainly if we don't capitalize on this golden opportunity and engage in, fund and fully support more research and an unprecedented number of studies to find out why there are, per capita, fewer criminals and even fewer victims of crime.

So, you say you are still not convinced that you are much safer today than you were just five years ago. Here are the figures: From 1993 to last year, rates of violent crime nationally have fallen 27 percent to the lowest level in twenty-five years—when the Justice Department first began recording crime rates. Those old enough to remember the early '70s should ask themselves how much they worried about crime in 1973. There has also been a 32 percent drop in property crimes over the same period. More important, there has been a seven-year downturn nationally in homicides, with Minneapolis this year seeing the lowest number of killings in the city by mid-year since '84. Violent juvenile crime across the nation is also at its lowest level in thirteen years.

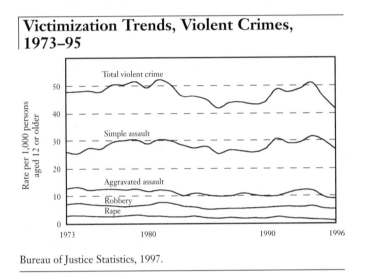

Victimization Trends, Violent Crimes, 1973–95

Bureau of Justice Statistics, 1997.

Still scared senseless over crime? Try turning off your TV. Your reality has probably become a deluge of sensationalized crime stories. If this is the case, it will take more than this article to dispel the myth generated by the media that crime rates move only in one direction. The simple and practical truth is, this downward trend in the crime rate deserves our attention, not because we can rest easy in our relative safety, but because at no other time have we been able to garner as much knowledge about why crime exists.

Why Crime Has Fallen

The task won't be easy. But there are discernible reasons for the falling crime rate. Some would argue that demographics and aging Baby Boomers play a significant role in the lower crime rate. While a larger and growing segment of society contends that incarcerating repeat, and even first-time, offenders for longer periods of time is having the greatest impact. Some scholars are suggesting that the decreasing crime rate and legalized abortion are correlated. Partisan politics would have you believe that the Clinton administration's crime prevention strategies of tougher sentencing, more prosecutions, and closer working relationships among law enforcement agencies are doing the job. Republicans remind us of anti-crime legislation that has been passed since the GOP gained control of Congress in '95. Locally, Minneapolis police point to the use of computers to map out developing crime zones as one factor that has reduced crime in the city. One of the likeliest reasons may be the nation's current economic prosperity.

Whether it has been one or all of these reasons, or even possibly some others, what we can be certain of is that because there are reasons for the lower crime rate, there also are viable solutions to crime.

But once this window of opportunity closes, it may be another quarter-century before we will again have such insights within reach. Worse yet, if we fail to discover the reasons now, once the beast is loose, our need to cage him again may cause us to resort to desperate and socially destructive actions.

3

VIEWPOINT

"More and more children are murdering their fellow children."

Youth Violence Is a Serious Problem

Bill Owens

In the following viewpoint, Bill Owens, the governor of Colorado, contends that youth violence is a growing problem. He argues that society must search for answers in order to understand why events like the Columbine High School shooting occur, and how those tragedies can be prevented. According to Owens, among the reasons for the increase in youth violence is violent movies, a lack of father figures, and schools that let unruly children disrupt the learning process.

As you read, consider the following questions:

1. How many cases of rape were reported at public schools during the 1996–97 school year, according to Owens?
2. Of children who brought guns to schools what percentage were prosecuted, as stated by the author?
3. Why does Owens not favor passing more legislation to end youth violence?

Excerpted from Bill Owens, governor of Colorado, a speech delivered to a summit on the Prevention of Youth Violence and School Safety, Denver, CO, June 19, 1999. Reprinted with permission.

More than two million children under the age of 18 are arrested each year—32% of them under the age of 15. Youth gang violence activity in Denver has more than doubled since 1979. Public schools across the country reported for the 1996–97 school year alone 4,000 cases of rape or other sexual battery and 11,000 incidents of physical attacks or fights where weapons were used.

A Long-Standing Problem

But more than anything, we gather today [at a Summit on the Prevention of Youth Violence and School Safety] because we as a society are scared. We, are scared that something has gone profoundly wrong in our state and in our nation. More and more children are murdering their fellow children. Friends, it grieves me to say that in this wonderful state of ours, children murder.

Unfortunately, it did not start on April 20th—that day was just one of the most concentrated and extreme examples of youth violence. More often, the violence happens one child killer and one child victim at a time. Sadly, it has become all too common—so common that at times it seems not to shock us—for children under the age of 18 to assault, rape and even murder.

Many of you in this room have spent years and devoted your lives to finding ways to reduce youth violence. We have grassroots leaders here that work one child at a time on the issues surrounding gangs, drugs, alienation and violence that afflict all too many children. We are here to discuss the whole breadth of issues surrounding youth violence and school safety—not just one horrific and tragic episode. For too many years, our children in the inner cities have been plagued by the problem of youth violence.

But we would do a disservice to the victims and families—and to the tens of millions of Americans who joined all of us in Colorado in our grief and in our search for answers—if we did not acknowledge that Columbine seemed to change things. The President spoke about it "piercing the soul of America." Others have called it a watershed event. Only time will tell.

But I hope that the evil that occurred this spring was the

straw that finally broke the camel's back. As is said about people fighting addiction —sometimes you have to hit bottom before truly committing yourself to recovery. I pray that Columbine was the worst it will ever get—and that now Colorado will lead the nation in recovery and turn the tide on youth violence.

We Must Do What Is Right

It was Edmund Burke who said that all that is necessary for evil to triumph is for good people to do nothing. And humans being humans, sometimes we find it easier to do nothing than to do what is right.

It can be easier to let our kids go to violent movies and play violent video games rather than argue with them about why it is not all right even though all their friends do it.

It can be easier to let our teenage boys spend hours in their rooms on the Internet doing Lord knows what—because supposedly all their friends do it.

It can be easier to go to the gym at the end of the day rather than find the time to mentor a young, fatherless boy who is desperate for someone to teach him the ways of manhood. And in that absence it is all too easy for that teenager to turn to gangs and to violence for affirmation.

Friends, America is full of good people. The vast majority of us work hard and try to provide for our families as best we can. The fact that we are all gathered here today shows that we are people willing to spend a Saturday discussing ways to rescue Colorado's children from violence.

None of us are perfect. There are no perfect solutions to youth violence. But we cannot let complacency get the best of us.

We cannot pretend that we do not know about the subculture of violence and death that haunts popular movies, music and video games—and is gobbled up by our children.

We cannot pretend that we do not know about children being raised with no sense of the value of human life—and thus think nothing of teenage parents throwing their newborn infant into the trash.

We cannot pretend that too many of our schools no longer seem to be founded and controlled by adults for the benefit of children. Too often we allow an unruly child to disrupt the learning of the other 25 students in a classroom yet when we don't remove the misbehaving child, we are saying to the other 24 children that respect for the rights of others doesn't matter.

John Branch. Reprinted with permission from John Branch and San Antonio Express News.

In the past two years, more than 6,000 young people were caught in schools with guns. Yet of those 6,000, only 13 were prosecuted. Think about that for a moment. Less than one-half of one-one-hundredth percent of the children who brought guns to school were prosecuted. That is not zero tolerance toward weapons in schools. No one would think of taking a gun to an airport—and if they did, they know they'd be prosecuted. We have zero tolerance toward weapons at our airports. Why don't we have the same attitude at our schools?

Finding a Solution

Time and again since April 20th, I've been asked about what we can do to stop children from murdering children. And time and again I've thought: If I could simply sign a piece of legislation that would stop the killing, I would obviously do so in an instant.

Unfortunately it is not that easy. The killers at Columbine broke dozens of laws against murder, assault, possession of guns, destruction of property. One more law—or a hundred new laws—wouldn't have stopped them. But if laws are not the answer, then where do we start? Do we blame it on parental indifference, violent movies, the Internet, dysfunctional schools, or some other cause?

I do not have all the answers and I do not pretend to know all the solutions. None of us do. But . . . we will ask questions and seek to learn from people who have spent years fighting against youth violence and working for safe schools. We will not discover a magic cure today, but I hope that we will find some concrete steps that we can take toward reducing youth violence.

Because together, we can begin to find our way, day by day. We will not stop the tide of violence overnight because we did not get into this overnight. It has happened little by little over the past 30 years.

"In the last 10 to 20 years, the rate of serious, violent crime has risen faster . . . among adults than among teens."

The Problem of Youth Violence Is Overstated

Michael A. Males

In the following viewpoint, Michael A. Males contends that violence is more likely to be committed by adults than by teenagers. He asserts that politicians who want to make scapegoats out of juveniles and pass harsher laws to punish juvenile criminals ignore statistics that show adult violent crime is increasing. According to Males, implementing curfews and executing juveniles who commit capital crimes will not reduce violence because such practices do not target the true problem, adult violence. Males is a sociologist and the author of *Framing Youth: Ten Myths About the New Generation.*

As you read, consider the following questions:
1. According to the author, what myths led to anti-youth extremism?
2. Between 1985 and 1995, by how much did felony-violence arrest rates rise among 30- to 39-year-olds, according to crime reports?
3. Why does Males criticize Ed Humes?

Excerpted from Michael A. Males, "Scapegoating Kids: The Myths About Youth Violence," *Oakland Tribune,* May 16, 1997. Reprinted with permission from the author.

If [former] California Gov. Pete Wilson and Assembly Speaker Cruz Bustamante's bipartisan willingness to consider executing 13-year-olds doesn't shock crime authorities into rethinking a decade of myth-making about "youth violence," what will it take?

Teenagers Are Committing Fewer Crimes

Experts familiar with state and federal crime reports know the politically unpalatable truths: In the last 10 to 20 years, the rate of serious, violent crime has risen faster (much faster in California) among adults than among teens. The rapid growth in teenage violence from 1985 to 1990, particularly homicide, occurred among minorities and was tied to poverty among nonwhite youth. Since 1990, teenage violent crime of all types, especially murder, in California has fallen while adult violent crime continues to rise.

The most baffling mystery is why grown-up violence—especially felony assault by middle-aged whites—is mushrooming, while crime is declining among destitute, inner-city teens. But such mysteries are not what politicians seeking easy scapegoats want to emphasize. So politically attuned experts evade basic points, such as surging adult violence or that a youth is three times more likely to be murdered by an adult than by another youth.

Accordingly, politicians extol get-tough panaceas, including executing ever-younger offenders, as (regrettably) necessary to save society from the coming horde of "adolescent super-predators."

No other Western nation puts juveniles to death. By contrast, the United States has executed 300—125 of them age 16 or younger, nearly all of them black. Since 1979, Amnesty International reports, 14 youths have been executed worldwide: nine in the United States, the others in Pakistan, Rwanda, Bangladesh and Barbados.

The latter nations have since outlawed juvenile executions, but U.S. politicians vie to string up eighth-graders considered too young to smoke a last cigarette. Only in the United States could the liberal concept of "crime prevention," now bandied about in Sacramento, mean punishing youths ever more harshly for curfew violations while ignoring the growing poverty, parental violence and adult drug abuse that make home the most dangerous place for kids to be.

The route to America's anti-youth extremism was paved largely with myths concocted by well-intentioned scholars. To defuse racist stereotypes hurled at poor people and minority groups, scholars proclaimed that rising savagery is innate to all teenagers, regardless of income or background.

But the claim that "kids everywhere" are more violent is plain wrong. Violent crime and murder rates among California's 2 million white teens are no higher today than 10 or 20 years ago. Nearly all California's growth in youth violence arrests occurred among minorities.

Failure to confront that uncomfortable reality has led to evasion of even more troubling issues: California's aging white majority is less and less inclined to support funding for schools, universities and social services for the rising nonwhite young at levels as high as those provided previous generations; blocking traditional education and employment pathways for today's poorer youth to escape poverty, and leading to the increasing management of young nonwhite men by police and prisons. Authorities and the media can peddle the fiction that youth violence and the legal system are egalitarian, but the reality is that 90% of California's teenage murder arrestees and a similar proportion of its imprisoned juveniles are nonwhite.

The Truth About Violence

History shows that violence is not inherent in age or race. Rather, it is tied to the stresses of economic adversity. Violence exploded during the Great Depression. Murder peaked in 1933–34 among all races, at levels well above those of 1995–96. The same pattern holds today. Fresno, California's poorest major county, suffers violent crime rates double those of Ventura, one of the state's richest, among whites, nonwhites, young, old, male and female alike. One thing these two very different counties (combined population 1.5 million) share: None of the 25 teens arrested for murder in 1995 was white.

Wilson and other authorities broadcast the single worst falsehood of today's crime debate: Teenage violence has skyrocketed while adult violence is stable. In fact, state crime reports clearly show that, from 1985 to 1995, felony-violence arrest rates rose by 58% among 20- to 29-year-olds; 114% among 30- to 39-year-olds, and 109% among middle-aged (40- to 69-year-olds) people—all far higher than the 38% increase among teens. A doubling in adults' serious violence in 10 years is a bizarre notion of "stable."

The Profiling Trend

Profiling for criminal tendencies, especially among students, is gaining ground. Thousands of people, afraid their sons might be potential killers, sought out the checklist of characteristics of young people prone to school violence provided by the National School Safety Center in California, which monitors lethal action in the schools. Among things to watch for in a child: "Mood swings. Loves violent television. Uses drugs or alcohol. Fond of bad language, name-calling and cursing. Is often depressed. Likes guns and blowing things up. Anti-social."

The problem with "trouble signs" is, they could fit most boys on a bad day and some on a good day.

Douglas Dennis, *Angolite*, May/June 1999.

The drumbeat of alarm by experts, such as Northeastern University's James Alan Fox, that more teenagers, whom he calls "temporary sociopaths," portend a "coming crime storm" is obsolete. The "crime storm" is here, but most of it is adult and much of it occurs in the home.

Author Ed Humes, who opposes the execution of teens, exemplifies the pitfall of demonizing adolescents while advocating more compassion. His recent study of L.A. juvenile justice, "No Matter How Loud I Shout," depicts the entire younger generation as berserk—"children killing children, violently, inhumanly, forcing one another to duck bullets, spraying whole crowds in order to take out a single intended victim." Nowhere does Humes use such inflammatory language to decry the far more common inhumanity of "adults killing children." (Ironically, of the two cases of "children killing children" he dramatizes, one involved adults shooting a youth, the other a wrongly accused teenage suspect).

Humes repeats the myth that adult violence is stable and reduces crucial issues of race and poverty to footnotes.

Creating Policy from Distorted Statistics

What result did Humes, the news media and liberal crime theorists expect from their endless teen-mayhem barrage? More child-friendly judges and midnight basketball, or public and politicians howling to punish these pre-pubescent psychopaths? Recent polls and focus groups show that adults, nationally and locally, believe youths commit three to five times more violent crime than they actually do. How can rational policy emerge from such a misconception?

It can't. The price of official distortion is policy futility. President Clinton and Wilson proclaim a "scourge of youth violence," while nationwide and in California, teenage crime rates and trends are strikingly similar to those of grown-ups of their sex, race and era. How can nostrums such as curfews (which, as Clinton proposes, would allow teens in public only a couple of hours on most days) and "taking guns away from kids" succeed when three-fourths of all murders involving youths also involve adult assailants?

No amount of cops, courts, prisons and death rows can solve the justifiable bitterness that underlies the isolation of the growing hundreds of thousands of impoverished youth from larger society, nor the family violence and drug abuse afflicting rising numbers of households, rich and poor alike. Confronting these realities is the job evaded by the same politicians now itching to pull the switch.

> "*[Thirty-two] percent of the 3,419 women killed in the United States in 1998, . . . died at the hands of a husband, a former husband, a boyfriend, or a former boyfriend.*"

Domestic Violence Against Women Is a Serious Problem

Erica Goode

Domestic violence against women—in particular, the murder of women by their current or former intimate partner—is a serious problem, asserts Erica Goode in the following viewpoint. She notes that although homicide rates are declining overall, the rate of decrease has not been as sharp for women who are murdered by a former or current husband or boyfriend. Goode maintains that homicides committed by intimate partners share certain traits, including being especially brutal and typically occurring within one year after the woman has separated from her partner. Goode also contends that women are more likely to be murdered if there has been a history of violence in the domestic relationship. Goode is a writer for *The New York Times*.

As you read, consider the following questions:
1. Why are men more likely to kill their partners, according to Goode?
2. As explained by the author, how can a man stalk a woman with whom he lives?
3. According to Sally Goldfarb, as cited by the author, what are some potentially dangerous gestures or comments that women should take as warning signs?

They had little or nothing in common. And in the normal course of events, it is unlikely their worlds would ever have intersected.

Three Homicidal Attacks

Kathleen A. Roskot, 19, the daughter of middle-class parents on Long Island, was a star athlete on the Columbia University lacrosse team. Marie Jean-Paul, 39, known to her friends as Carol, grew up in Haiti, and worked as a nurse's aide at a hospital in Brooklyn. Joy Thomas, 18, graduated from Mount Vernon High School in June and was studying to be a teacher at Westchester Community College.

Yet in the course of 48 hours, the lives of these three women were abruptly and horribly linked together: they were, all three, the targets of homicidal attacks by men with whom they had had romantic relationships.

On February 6, Ms. Roskot's throat was slashed in her dormitory room with a kitchen knife, apparently wielded by a former Columbia student she had dated. The next morning in Brooklyn, Mrs. Jean-Paul's husband used a machete to cut his wife's throat, then doused her body and set it on fire.

Ms. Thomas, shot in the head in Westchester hours later, lived, but only through a stroke of luck: her former boyfriend's pistol jammed. In all three cases, the men believed responsible for the attacks committed suicide shortly afterward.

Such events ought to be surprising. In fact, anyone who examines the crime reports knows that they are commonplace.

Homicides by Intimate Partners

According to homicide statistics collected by the Federal Bureau of Investigation, 32 percent of the 3,419 women killed in the United States in 1998, the latest year for which data are available, died at the hands of a husband, a former husband, a boyfriend or a former boyfriend.

On the basis of smaller, regional studies and the limitations of the data gathering methods used by the F.B.I., however, many experts believe that the true figure is much higher, perhaps as much as 50 percent to 70 percent. In comparison, 4 percent of 10,606 male homicide victims in 1998 were killed by current or former intimate partners.

And while homicide rates as a whole have sharply declined over the past 20 years, and the rate at which men are killed by intimate partners along with them, rates for women, and particularly for white women, have not declined as sharply, despite efforts by police departments around the country to increase their response to calls involving domestic violence. In some regions, New York City for example, they have not gone down at all.

"We haven't come close to affecting intimate partner violence and homicide the way we have other kinds of violence and assault," said Dr. Susan Wilt, director of the New York City Department of Health's Office of Health Promotion and Disease Prevention. "It remains a shocking issue that this is the main reason that women end up dead and that it occurs within the context of their home and family, where they are supposed to be safe."

"Women worry when they go out," Dr. Wilt said. "They should worry when they stay in."

Why Their Murders Occur

Why are men so much more likely to kill their partners than women? Feminist scholars and domestic violence experts have long contended that such crimes reflect a society in which men feel entitled to exercise power and control over women, and to use physical violence when necessary to assert their dominance.

"We are in a culture that in many ways celebrates male dominance and female submission, and that is in some ways the definition of an erotic heterosexual relationship," said Sally Goldfarb, an associate professor at Rutgers School of Law in Camden, N.J., and an expert in family law.

Some evolutionary psychologists who study spousal murders, like Dr. Margo Wilson and Dr. Martin Daly at McMaster University in Ontario, also argue that men as a whole, rather than individual men, are the problem. But they base this assertion not on culture but on biology. Violence, they believe, may have developed as a strategy for men to exert proprietary control over women, and in particular over their reproductive capacities. Many psychologists, in contrast, focus on the personality characteristics and life histories that lead men to batter and kill.

Whatever the validity of such views, social scientists have in recent years begun to investigate homicides by intimate partners in a much more systematic way, hoping to find ways to spot the potential for lethal violence before it occurs, and to develop better tactics for intervention.

What emerges from such studies is a picture as consistent as it is discomforting. Many studies confirm, for example, that women are at particular risk when they are in the process of leaving a relationship, something long noted by domestic violence workers.

In a study of 293 women killed by intimates in North Carolina from 1991 to 1993, Dr. Beth Moracco of the University of North Carolina School of Public Health and her colleagues found that 42 percent had been killed after they threatened separation, tried to separate or had recently separated from their partners. In another study, researchers found that of 551 intimate partner homicides in Ontario from 1974 to 1990, 32 percent were committed in the context of a separation; in another 11 percent, the killer believed that the female partner was sexually unfaithful.

The period just after a woman has left is often the most risky, studies find. In a review of homicides in Chicago, for example, Dr. Wilson and Dr. Daly found that 50 percent of the killings of wives by their husbands took place within two months of a separation; 85 percent occurred within a year.

"The link between separation and murder is more than incidental," Dr. Wilson and Dr. Daly observed in their study. "Homicidal husbands are often noted to have threatened to do exactly what they did, should their wives ever leave them, and they often explain their homicides as responses to the intolerable stimulus of the wife's departure."

Intensely Violent Murders

The intensity of emotion that leads men to kill women they once loved is often evident in the crimes themselves.

"It's absolutely a crime of rage," said Dr. Wilt, who has been tracking homicides by intimate partners in New York City since 1990. "There is a sense of 'How dare you think you can live without me?'"

Of the 379 women known to have been killed by male intimates in New York from 1990 to 1997, Dr. Wilt and her colleagues found, 46.7 percent were killed with guns, 26.6 percent were stabbed, 8.2 percent were bludgeoned, 7.9 percent were strangled, and 10.6 percent were killed by other means, including suffocation and being pushed from a window or the top of a building.

That women killed by a male partner are more likely to be stabbed or strangled than those killed by someone less close to them, Dr. Wilt said, reflects the emotional nature of the crime. "When you stab or strangle someone to death, it's a lot more intimate than shooting them," Dr. Wilt said.

Characteristics of Domestic Violence Victims

Race is one of the factors that determine the chances a woman will be the victim of intimate violence. African-American women are more likely than women of other races to be victimized, as are women who live in urban areas. Intimate victimization affects younger women (ages 16–24) most frequently. Moreover, the classlessness of domestic violence is a myth, because victims also tend to be poor, with family incomes under $7,000. It may be, however, that victimization of lower income women is more likely to be reported to the police, since women with higher incomes and more status in the community have the resources to deal with domestic violence privately without involving the criminal justice system.

Domestic violence is also associated with low marriage rates, high unemployment, and social problems, and, according to the intervention providers interviewed for this report, women in cross-cultural relationships may also be at unusually high risk. The last factor may be due to cultural differences in expectations about sex roles and acceptable behavior.

Kerry Murphy Healey and Christine Smith, *National Institute of Justice*, July 1998.

Dr. Donald Dutton, a psychologist at the University of British Columbia, who recently completed a study of 50 men in prison for killing their wives, said that "typically, the murder itself is overkill—there is more done to the woman than is necessary to kill her."

Dr. Dutton said men who killed their wives or girlfriends

tended to fall into two categories. A minority, he said, are calculating killers, whose motive is instrumental: cashing in on an insurance policy, for example. More common, he said, are killers who suffer from severe personality disturbances. Such men, Dr. Dutton said, often have a terror of being abandoned and express their dependency in extreme jealousy and controlling behavior.

"What's going on deep down is that they believe the woman is leaving them and they can't live without her," he said. "The prospect of her leaving throws them into a downward spiral where they feel like they are staring into the abyss."

Frequently, Dr. Dutton added, the killer enters a "dissociated," trancelike state after the killing. In one case, he said, a man killed his wife and children in Berkeley, California, boarded a plane for New York, and was picked up by the police at La Guardia Airport still wearing his bloody clothes.

Sometimes when a woman is murdered, it appears to come out of nowhere: Thomas G. Nelford, the Columbia dropout who is believed to have killed Ms. Roskot, appears to have had no history of battering, and friends described him as a pacifist.

Risk Factors for Violence

More often, though, there were many portents of danger. Through a study of completed and attempted murders of women by intimate partners in 11 large and mid-size cities, a group of researchers, led by Dr. Jacquelyn Campbell at Johns Hopkins University School of Nursing, is trying to put together a list of risk factors for lethal violence.

The study is not yet completed, but Dr. Campbell and her colleagues have published a small part of their findings and have posted some preliminary findings on the Internet.

The study reinforces the findings of other research. For example, Dr. Campbell said in an interview, the researchers are finding that the biggest risk factor is a history of violent behavior by the man in the relationship. Of 250 women in the study who were killed by current or former partners, 65 percent had been assaulted by their partners in the past. Of the 200 victims of attempted homicide, 72 percent had experienced a previous assault.

Past stalking of the woman by her male partner, Dr. Campbell and her colleagues found, also posed a significant risk, occurring in 69 percent of homicides and 84 percent of attempted homicides. When the woman had separated from her partner, the frequency of stalking rose to 88 percent.

In many cases, Dr. Campbell said, stalking occurred even when the couple lived together. A man, for example, might show up unexpectedly at his partner's workplace, beep her repeatedly on a pager, demanding to know where she is, or telephone her dozens of times a day.

Other predictors of lethal violence included an escalation in the frequency or severity of physical abuse, attempts by the man to choke the woman or to force her to have sex, the presence of a gun in the house, the use of street drugs or the abuse of alcohol by the man, verbal threats, and the woman's belief that her partner was capable of killing her.

A history of domestic violence is found less often in men who kill themselves after killing their partners, Dr. Campbell said. Studies indicate that about 25 percent of men who kill their partners commit suicide afterward. Often, they do so with an equal display of emotion: Mrs. Jean-Paul's husband, for example, is believed to have set himself on fire. The man police believe killed Ms. Roskot threw himself in front of a subway train a few hours after she was killed.

Curiously, in the multicity study, men who tortured or killed animals—long thought to be a sign of potential danger—were no more likely to kill their partners. But Dr. Campbell cautioned: "No matter what the research says, what I say to women is, 'If he does something that is terribly frightening, be scared! If it makes the hair stand up on the back of your neck, be scared!'"

In one case she encountered, Dr. Campbell said, a man slit the throat of his wife's favorite dog and left the dead pet in the bathtub for her to find.

Danger Signs

What can women do to protect themselves? At least one study, by the National Center for State Courts, of civil protection orders issued in three jurisdictions, found that contrary to popular belief, such orders are effective in the majority of cases, making women feel safer and reducing incidents of violence. A court order obtained by Ms. Thomas, the Westchester Community College student, however, appears to have done her little good.

Still, in most cases, by the time a court intervenes, the woman's situation is already dire. For young women, said Ms. Goldfarb of Rutgers, an important preventive measure is to be alert for signs that a man is potentially dangerous—before the relationship grows serious.

"Many of the same types of gestures or comments that we are taught as young girls to view as romantic are, in fact, major warning signs of a serious potential for domestic violence," Ms. Goldfarb said.

She gave as examples statements that might appear solicitous but that in reality may indicate extreme jealousy or a controlling nature. A man might say, for example, "I can't live without you," or "You only need me," or "I can't breathe unless I'm near you." Or he might phone her 20 times a day or appear unexpectedly at her door.

"It may sound like Prince Charming," Ms. Goldfarb said. "But in reality that kind of possessiveness is designed to isolate a woman from other sources of support in her life. It is a foreshadowing of violence."

And perhaps a signal to stay as far away as possible.

> "*Soon after the first battered women found
> safe haven in the feminist movement,
> researchers began to reveal that violence in
> the home actually claimed victims of both
> sexes.*"

Domestic Violence Against Men
Is a Serious Problem

Patricia Pearson

In the following viewpoint, Patricia Pearson claims that domestic violence against men is a serious problem that is being ignored. She argues that domestic violence perpetrated by women is viewed skeptically because, unlike female victims, men often suffer no visible injuries. In addition, Pearson asserts that many feminists have attacked or ignored the findings of people who study the issue of female-initiated domestic violence. Pearson is a crime journalist and the author of *When She Was Bad: Violent Women & the Myth of Innocence*, the book from which this viewpoint has been excerpted.

As you read, consider the following questions:

1. According to the author, how were battered women treated before the 1970s?
2. What fraction of relationships had an exclusively violent female, according to a 1985 study cited by Pearson?
3. According to Michael Thomas, as cited by Pearson, what type of men often permit assaults against them?

Most of us believe that masculine power is the fountain-head of private, as well as public, violence. Spouse assault is what *men* do to *women*, women from all walks of life, getting punched in the face by the dark fist of patriarchy. Even if we concede that women batter their children, we cannot take it a step further and picture them battering men. We might learn that a man's nose was broken, that he lost his job, that he was emotionally devastated, but we still think to ourselves: He's a man. He could have hit back. He could have hit *harder*.

On the whole, men do indeed have a more powerful left hook. The problem is that the dynamic of domestic violence is not analogous to two differently weighted boxers in a ring. There are relational strategies and psychological issues at work in an intimate relationship that negate the fact of physical strength. At the heart of the matter lies human will. Which partner—by dint of temperament, personality, life history—has the will to harm the other? By now it should be clear that such a will is not the exclusive province of men. If it were, we wouldn't have the news coming out of North America's gay community that violence by women against women in personal relationships occurs with a frequency approaching violence in heterosexual relationships—with the smaller, more conventionally feminine partner often being the one who strikes.

A great source of skepticism for people confronting the concept of husband assault is the absence of visible injury. Few abused men or lesbians emerge from their relationships resembling Hedda Nussbaum, the New Yorker whose common-law husband, Joel Steinberg, was prosecuted in 1988 for the beating death of their adopted daughter, Lisa. When Hedda Nussbaum testified, her appallingly broken face, with its cauliflower ear and boxer nose, was so vividly captured by television cameras that she quickly became the iconographic figure of the battered woman. Every time an activist proclaimed that one in four American women were assaulted by their partners, the image of Nussbaum sprang to mind.

In reality, victims like Hedda Nussbaum dwell at the extreme end of a continuum of violence in marital and dating relationships, in which about 4 percent of women are that severely injured. The majority of couples embroiled in intimate power struggles engage in a spectrum of violent acts, which women are statistically as likely as men to initiate: the slaps across the face, the glass suddenly hurled, the bite, the fierce pinch, the waved gun, the kick to the stomach, the knee to the groin. Add the invisible wave of violence that washes over American households in an acid bath of words, the children used as pawns, the destruction of property, the enlistment of community as a means of control, and all this paints a much more complex picture of domestic violence than that summoned by one woman's face in a heartbreaking trial.

That we have not been able to get at this complexity, in terms of the range of behavior, its causes, and its victims, has everything to do with how the issue evolved in the popular mind to begin with. Spousal assault was once a silent crime. The violence was private, like child assault. What people did behind closed doors was the business neither of their neighbors nor of the state. The first radical alteration of this paradigm came about in the early 1970s, through the work of Second Wave feminists. Because they were concentrating on the problems of women—transforming what were once considered personal issues into political concerns— they exposed the female victims of domestic assault. The subject made headlines with the publication of *Battered Wives* by the journalist Del Martin in 1976, one year after Susan Brownmiller opened the door on rape with her landmark book *Against Our Will.*

The first order of business, for many feminists like Martin, was to remove the stigma attached to battered women. Prior to *Battered Wives,* the few investigations that had been made into battery had been conducted by court-appointed male psychiatrists who were asked to assess male assailants for trial. Since the assailants refused to concede any problem, the psychiatrists refocused their attention on the wives who'd been assaulted and, in the grand tradition of pathologizing female behavior, came up with a host of victim-blaming labels: "masochists," "castrators," "flirts." From the outset of claiming this issue for women, it was critical to clear battered women of blame. As this mission gained momentum, with more and more women testifying about their experiences to feminists and journalists, the need to shield victims from blame gained currency. To pose the question "Why did she stay?" quickly became unacceptable. It emerged that there were a number of reasons why women stayed—for the sake of their children, or because of financial dependency, or because, even if they left, their husbands would track them down. Most people accepted such reasons as credible, as evidenced most recently by the funds allotted in 1994 by the United States federal Violence Against Women Act. Male approval of spousal assault has dropped 50 percent in this period, from 20 percent of men thinking it's acceptable to strike your wife to 10.

Soon after the first battered women found safe haven in the feminist movement, research began to reveal that violence in the home actually claimed victims of both sexes. The most significant data came from a survey published in 1980 by three highly respected family violence scholars in New Hampshire, Murray Straus, Richard Gelles, and Suzanne Steinmetz. Their random survey of 3,218 American homes uncovered that severe abuse was committed equally by men and women. Minor, but recurring, violence was also on a par, with 11.6 percent of women and 12 percent of men reporting that they hit, slapped, or kicked their partners.

Attacks on Male Victims

At this point, people working on the subject of family violence had a choice. They could expand the field to include male victims—establishing that abused men were not the same men who were abusing, and vice versa for women—or they could do what they did: devote an extraordinary amount of energy to shouting male victims down. For feminists, the idea that men could be victimized was nonsensical. It didn't square with their fundamental analysis of wife assault—that it was an extension of male political, economic, and ideological dominance over women. If women were so clearly subjugated in the public domain, through rape, sexual harassment, job discrimination, and so on, how could there be a different reality behind closed doors? Activists anticipated, moreover, that the New Hampshire data might be used to devalue female victims, in the manner of male lawyers, judges, and politicians saying, "See? She does it too"; case dismissed.

As a result, critics rushed to accuse Straus and Gelles, who were the primary authors, of shoddy research. They argued that their measurement tools were "patriarchal" and that they hadn't explored the context of the violence: If women were equally abusive, it was only in self-defense. None could assert this as fact; nor did they criticize the lack of context for assaults against women. On the contrary, the Straus/Gelles survey method (called the conflict tactics scale) was quickly adopted as a tool for research into violence against women. But Straus and Gelles, put on the defensive, re-worked their survey questions and sampled several thousand households again. Their findings, published in 1985, were virtually identical, with the additional discovery that women initiated the aggression as often as men. About a quarter of the relationships had an exclusively violent male, another quarter had an exclusively violent female, and the rest were mutually aggressive.

Once again, there was a flurry of protest and scrutiny. Scholars set out to prove that male self-esteem was less damaged by abuse, that men took their wives' violence less seriously, and that injury had to be measured in terms of harm rather than intentions. A woman with a broken jaw could not be compared to a man like Peter Swann, who only got an ashtray to the head. In truth, both sides were guilty of using a male-centered measure of harm, in that neither was looking at the damage women could cause through indirect aggression. Moreover, Straus and Gelles, as well as subsequent scholars, have found that men often do, in fact, sustain comparable levels of injury. A 1995 study of young American military couples, arguably the most patriarchal of all, found that 47 percent of the husbands and wives had bruised, battered, and wounded each other to exactly the same degree. The argument about harm versus intention has been confounded in recent years, at any rate, by the addition of "mental" and "emotional" abuse to the lexicon of female victimization. A spate of new books on the self-help market argue that verbal abuse damages women as badly as physical blows. Picking up on this theme, California has added new provisions to its prisoner clemency policy, allowing women to apply for release for killing their mates due to "emotional" abuse. Since nobody can sensibly argue that women aren't capable of extremely artful and wounding verbal attacks (studies find high degrees of female verbal hostility in violent marriages), the whole question of "harm" gets turned on its head.

Abused Men Are Mocked and Ignored

There is little sympathy for a man who is attacked by his wife. On the Oregon coast, a woman was accused of sneaking up on her newlywed husband and bludgeoning him with a tire iron. The state's largest newspaper treated the incident as high entertainment, with the headline HUSBAND SURVIVES THE LUMPS AND BUMPS OF A NEW MARRIAGE, but readers found a decidedly unfunny story of a man with broken fingers from trying to ward off the blows of a brutal attack. The wife was later convicted of attempted murder and sentenced to several years in prison. It was alleged she had tried to murder him for his money.

Men assaulted by their wives may find a complete lack of services. In a study on domestic police calls in Detroit, one man was hospitalized after his wife stabbed him in the chest, barely missing his lungs. Not only did the police refuse to arrest her; they wouldn't even remove her from the home.

Rene Denfeld, *Kill the Body, the Head Will Fall*, 1997.

Nevertheless, battered women's supporters are so invested in a gender dichotomy that some have even stooped to attacking male victim researchers on a personal level. After Suzanne Steinmetz proposed the battered husband syndrome in an article published in 1978 in *Victimology*, a speech she was asked by the ACLU to give was canceled because the organization received a bomb threat. Steinmetz also received so many threatening phone calls at home that she had to get an unlisted number. Thirteen years later, in 1991, the chairwoman of a Canadian panel on violence against women, Pat Marshall, when asked if she was familiar with the Straus/Gelles studies, replied that she was familiar with Murray Straus as a man and insinuated that he abused his wife. Marshall repeated these comments so frequently that Straus had to write to the Canadian minister responsible for the status of women to request a public apology. He received one. His wife, the pawn in this pretty maneuver, did not.

Accompanying the resistance to statistics on men has been a tendency to suppress data altogether. A 1978 survey conducted by the Kentucky Commission on Violence Against Women uncovered that 38 percent of the assaults in the state were committed by women, but that finding wasn't included when the survey was released. (The information was discovered some years later by scholars.) In Detroit, a tally of emergency medical admissions due to domestic violence was widely reported by activists as evidence of injuries to women. No one told the media that 38 percent of the admissions were men. In Canada, the federal government allotted $250,000 to a research project on comparative rates of violence in dating relationships. The lead researcher, Carleton University sociologist Walter DeKeseredy, released his data on women, generating a wave of violence against women headlines and conveying the impression that Canadian college campuses were bastions of violent misogyny. DeKeseredy didn't mention in his report that he had collected evidence of dating violence against men. If his data, which he intends to publish in 1997, reflect most other studies on dating violence, the rates will be equal. Physical aggression by young women in premarital romance is among the best documented.

"The battered husband syndrome is a backlash," DeKeseredy said in a 1994 telephone interview. "Men are using this information to keep women out of shelters." In fact, men are not using the information for anything, because academics with a particular political agenda are keeping it to themselves.

Under the circumstances, it is not surprising that those who stumble across evidence of battered men and battered lesbians do so quite by accident. A Winnipeg social scientist named Reena Sommer conducted a citywide survey on alcoholism for the University of Manitoba in 1989. Out of curiosity, she included six questions about domestic violence, interested specifically in violence against women. Some years later, she went back to her data and looked at the rates she'd collected on violence against men. To her astonishment, she found that 39.1 percent of the women in her survey had responded that they had committed acts of violence against their spouses at some point in their relationships, with 16.2 percent of those acts defined as severe. Sommer went back to her original list, found the telephone numbers, called up her respondents, and interviewed 737 of them. Ninety percent of the women who'd reported being abusive told her that they hadn't struck in self-defense. They had been furious or jealous, or they were high, or frustrated. Rational or irrational, impulsive or controlling, they had hit, kicked, thrown, and bitten. Fourteen percent of the men went to the hospital.

In Columbus, Ohio, two young sociologists, Laura Potts and Mary Reiter, were working in a "misdemeanor intake program" in the city attorney's office, criminal division, trying to settle minor charges through mediation, without bringing individuals to trial. Although nothing they'd read as feminists prepared them to expect it, they kept encountering men who'd been assaulted by women. One was an ailing, seventy-five-year-old man whose much younger wife had smashed him over the head with a porcelain vase. Another was a man attempting to break up with his girlfriend who got slashed in the temple with a screwdriver. In a third case, a man leaving his home to avoid an argument with his wife was chased down the street and stabbed in the back. "What we were seeing in reality," Potts told a meeting of the American Society of Criminology in 1994, "was a far greater use of [violence by women] than what we saw in the literature."

In Seattle, a therapist named Michael Thomas encountered the same gap between his schooling and his on-the-job experience. "My initial work was with a child abuse agency," he says. "When you start listening to the children's stories, you start to realize that there's an awful lot more violence by women than any of us had been trained to expect." Moving into private practice, Thomas began meeting "men who'd been sexually abused, often by their mothers." Within that distressing realm he heard his first accounts of husband abuse, for it is often men who witnessed or experienced violence in childhood who permit themselves to be assaulted as adults. As one battered husband who'd been abused in his boyhood explained: "We have not had control, as men, so we're not familiar with it and we're quite willing to give it over."

Periodical Bibliography

The following articles have been selected to supplement the diverse views presented in this chapter. Addresses are provided for periodicals not indexed in the *Readers' Guide to Periodical Literature*, the *Alternative Press Index*, the *Social Sciences Index*, or the *Index to Legal Periodicals and Books*.

Anonymous	"Going Underground," *Ms.*, February/March 2000.
Charles L. Baker	"Home Is Where the Violence Is," *Children's Voice*, Fall 1999. Available from Child Welfare League of America, 440 First St. NW, Third Floor, Washington, DC 20001-2085.
Alfred Blumstein and Richard Rosenfeld	"Assessing the Recent Ups and Downs in U.S. Homicide Rates," *National Institute of Justice Journal*, October 1998. Available from U.S. Department of Justice, Office of Justice Programs, National Institute of Justice, Washington, DC 20531.
Adam Cohen	"Special Report: Troubled Kids—Criminals as Copycats," *Time*, May 31, 1999.
Carey Goldberg and Marjorie Connelly	"Fear and Violence Have Declined Among Teenagers, Poll Shows," *The New York Times*, October 20, 1999.
Thomas Hine	"Teenagers and Crime," *American Heritage*, September 1999.
Issues and Controversies On File	"Domestic Violence," June 12, 1998. Available from Facts On File News Services, 11 Penn Plaza, New York, NY 10001.
Juvenile Justice Update	"A Report Card on School Crime and School Safety," December/January 1999. Available from Civic Research Institute, 4490 Route 27, PO Box 585, Kingston, NJ 08528.
Kathy Koch	"School Violence," *CQ Researcher*, October 9, 1998. Available from 1414 22nd St. NW, Washington, DC 20037.
Jennifer L. Pozner	"Not All Domestic Violence Studies Are Created Equal," *Extra!* November/December 1999.
Sue Anne Pressley	"Maybe It Can Happen Here," *Washington Post National Weekly Edition*, January 10, 2000.
Dennis Shepard	"My Son Matt," *Advocate*, April 30, 2000.
Nancy Updike	"Hitting the Wall," *Mother Jones*, May 1999.

What Are the Causes of Violence?

Chapter Preface

Nearly four out of every ten violent crimes has a common element. That link is not the race or age of the suspect but rather the fact that he or she was under the influence of alcohol at the time of the offense.

One type of violent crime that is associated with alcohol is domestic violence. According to the U.S. Department of Justice's Bureau of Justice Statistics, two-thirds of victims who experienced violence at the hands of a former or current romantic partner reported that alcohol was involved. In contrast, when the assailant was a stranger, only 31 percent of the victims perceived the assault to be alcohol-related. A study published in the *New England Journal of Medicine* in December 1999 reports that the risk of domestic violence more than triples if the male partner is an alcohol abuser.

According to the National Institute on Alcohol Abuse and Alcoholism, there are several explanations for why alcohol use can lead to violent crime and aggression. Alcohol is believed to disrupt the mechanisms in the brain that prevent impulsive behavior. The Institute explains: "Alcohol can also lead a person to misjudge social cues, thereby overreacting to a perceived threat." NIAAA also notes that people expect alcohol consumption to result in violence and cites research that shows that people who believe they have consumed alcohol—even when they have been given mock alcohol drinks—act more aggressively. Hence, social and cultural influences may be as important as biology in explaining the connection between alcohol and violence.

Some experts, however, warn that the link between alcohol and violence should not be overstated. The NIAAA notes that studies show that people who have been drinking rarely become more aggressive if they have not been provoked or threatened. Moreover, the National Crime Prevention Council argues that alcohol might not actually cause domestic violence but may simply be an excuse offered by an abusive domestic partner to explain his or her behavior.

What the research on alcohol and violence suggests, then, is that violence can be driven by a variety of forces. In the following chapter, the authors explore the causes of violence.

"*Any form of brain damage . . . can lead to recurrent violent behavior in previously peaceful individuals.*"

Brain Damage Can Cause Violence

Norbert Myslinski

In the following viewpoint, Norbert Myslinski contends that violent behavior is often the result of physical abnormalities in the brain. He argues that such brain dysfunction can be genetic or acquired later in life due to illness, injury, or a chemical imbalance. For example, Myslinski notes that low levels of the brain chemical serotonin are often associated with increased violence. He maintains that violent behavior can be controlled by regulating serotonin levels in affected individuals. Myslinski is an associate professor of neuroscience at the University of Maryland in Baltimore.

As you read, consider the following questions:
1. What is episodic dyscontrol, as defined by the author?
2. According to Myslinski, what are some of the mental drives that serotonin regulates?
3. According to the author, what experiences can influence serotonin production?

Reprinted from Norbert Myslinski, "Violence and the Brain," *The World & I*, May 1997. Reprinted with permission from *The World & I*, a publication of The Washington Times Corporation, copyright © 1997.

It began again, as it had hundreds of times before. Another uncontrollable rage. She started kicking and scratching and hitting anything and anyone in sight. Her foster parents had to hold her down for an hour until she was somewhat calmed. "This is the last time," they said. They had had enough. They finally decided to give up Rachel, as had other foster parents before them.

Rachel was nine years old, with a history of spontaneous, impulsive violence. Her psychiatrist labeled her as "attention deficit/hyperactive," a general term used to cover a wide range of abnormal behavior. Rachel was eventually hospitalized, but nothing helped to curb her violent behavior. Talk therapy, behavioral therapy, drug therapy—nothing worked, until she was given a drug that increased the levels of a chemical called *serotonin* in her brain.

The Effects of Brain Dysfunction

Neuroscientists have long known that violent behavior can be correlated with neuroanatomy (brain structure) and neurochemistry (brain chemistry). Brain dysfunction, either genetic or acquired, can result in a decreased ability to control one's violent tendencies. This fact, however, has been dwarfed in the public's mind by the cultural and societal causes of violence. In 1979, Gelles and Strauss listed 15 theories of violence. None of them included the brain. It is important that we not ignore the brain.

Can scientific research into the brain help us understand and prevent violence? Most neuroscientists who study violent behavior believe that their work offers no cure, no "magic pill," for most of the violence that plagues society. Some chronically violent people, however, may suffer from structural or chemical imbalance in their brains. Restoring the normal balance may reverse a lifelong pattern of violence.

The type of violence we will focus on here is called *episodic dyscontrol*—that is, impulsive, physical aggression with the intent to harm. We will not be concerned with collective violence, opportunistic or premeditated violence, or violence that results from psychotic illusions, delusions, or hallucinations.

Episodic dyscontrol refers to individuals whose attacks of rage appeared for the first time after a brain insult, or in whom it has been present since childhood or adolescence in association with other developmental defects. Individuals who possess this biological short fuse tend to act without fully considering the consequences.

Episodic dyscontrol is important because it is one of the causes of such acts as unpremeditated homicide, suicide, child abuse, spousal abuse, animal abuse, and property destruction. Sometimes it manifests itself as simply obscene and profane language, or excessively aggressive driving. The attacks can be triggered by the most trivial and impersonal of events. They are exacerbated by alcohol, usually followed by remorse.

Violence and the Cerebral Cortex

The ability to control our violent tendencies comes from our cerebral cortex, which is more complex than any other in the animal kingdom. It is the seat of our intelligence, creativity, and personal responsibility. Our brain also has an emotional center, called the limbic system. It is responsible for not only joy and affection but also fear and anger, which are the bases of most violent behavior. The control of our violent tendencies comes from inhibition of the limbic system by the cerebral cortex. While this control is active and healthy in most of us, it is lacking in many who commit violent crimes.

Just as damage to the brain can result in paralysis, chronic pain, mental retardation, or dementia, it may also result in loss of emotional control. Any form of brain damage, if it occurs in precisely the correct part of the brain, can lead to recurrent violent behavior in previously peaceful individuals. Possible causes of brain damage include trauma, tumors, stroke, brain infections such as encephalitis, or diseases that attack selective parts of the brain, such as multiple sclerosis or Alzheimer's disease. Among the best childhood predictors of violent behavior are neurological abnormalities. They include low IQ, attention deficit and hyperactivity, learning disabilities, head injuries, and prenatal and perinatal complications.

As far back as 1892, Dr. F.L. Goltz changed gentle dogs into vicious ones by removing part of their cerebral cortex. Since then, scientists have been able to turn an animal's rage on and off by stimulating certain parts of the brain. One of these parts is the *amygdala*, which is located in each temporal lobe.

Julie was a patient with epilepsy resulting from damage to her brain's temporal lobes. Besides seizures, she experienced sudden outbursts of anger. She once stabbed a woman who accidentally bumped into her. When Julie's physician inserted electrodes into the amygdala on both sides of her brain, he recorded abnormal activity from the right amygdala. To cure her, therefore, he destroyed her right amygdala by sending radio-frequency current through the electrode. Fifteen years later, she is still free of seizure activity and has no problem controlling her violent tendencies.

Attacks of aggressiveness are not uncommon in temporal lobe epileptics. Up to 50 percent of them exhibit impulsive violence between seizures. Vincent van Gogh suffered from the same condition, which led him to cut off part of his left earlobe with a razor.

Abnormalities in Violent Individuals

Numerous studies have shown that there is a higher prevalence of neurologic abnormalities in recurrently violent individuals than in nonviolent control subjects or the population at large. In one such study of 286 patients with episodic dyscontrol, 94 percent had neurological defects detectable by tests such as EEG or CAT scans. Most of the remaining 6 percent had one or more family members who exhibited explosive behavior, sometimes extending back two or three generations. One hundred and two patients exhibited initial violent episodes shortly after specific brain damage from head trauma, brain tumors, encephalitis, or stroke. All of the others had had violent episodes since childhood, and many of them had birth injuries. Although most of the patients had neurological defects, two-thirds of them were psychiatrically normal. Between violent attacks, they were indistinguishable from the normal population.

Just as brain damage can unleash violent behavior, in rare instances, damage can also subdue violent behavior. A 60-year-old man, who suffered from episodic dyscontrol since adolescence, experienced an abrupt personality change after a stroke. His uncontrollable rages stopped, and he became a gentler man. Another example is a woman with a brain tumor who reported as a first symptom the loss of a lifelong tendency to explosive behavior. The most dramatic example of controlling aggressiveness of an animal occurred in a bull-fight. Scientists were able to stop a charging bull in its tracks by remotely activating a stimulating electrode that was implanted in the bull's brain.

The above examples demonstrate neuroanatomical correlates of aggression. In other words, just as a specific part of the brain is responsible for the movement of a toe or the storage of a memory, a particular part of the brain is correlated with impulsive physical violence. There are also neurochemical correlates of aggression in the brain: Certain chemicals are correlated with violent behavior and others, with inhibiting it.

Low Serotonin Levels Can Cause Violence

Like normal body temperature, normal aggression has a set point, maintained by a delicate balance of brain chemicals. Changing that balance can either increase or decrease aggressiveness. A number of studies point to the involvement of a naturally occurring substance called serotonin. It is one of a number of neurotransmitters that relay messages between nerve cells and along pathways connecting different parts of the brain.

Serotonin is involved in pathways that help regulate some of our most basic mental drives—including sleep, pain, perception, sex, and, it now appears, our violent tendencies. Serotonin is an intricate part of the brain's impulse control system. If we lose it, we lose control. In both humans and animals, there is an inverse relationship between serotonin and violence: Low serotonin levels are associated with increased violence; high serotonin levels, with decreased violence.

Research has demonstrated this relationship in people incarcerated for violent crimes, marines discharged for excessive violence, and people who have attempted violent suicide. Serotonin levels are low in abused children. They are generally lower in males than in females. They tend to increase with age, which may be one reason why aggressive youths tend to mellow as they get older. Alcohol initially raises serotonin, but continued use reduces its levels. In one study of 29 children and adolescents with disruptive behavior disorders, low serotonin levels in the brain were the single most accurate predictor of which ones would go on to commit more violent crimes or suicide.

Responding to the Criminal Brain

As neuroscientists learn more about which parts of the brain seem to be associated with various aspects of behavior, social scientists, psychologists, and defense lawyers are using the same technologies to blame deviant or criminal behavior on the brain, instead of on the brain's owner. According to a *Time* cover story, a "breathtaking array of aberrant behaviors," including "severe alcoholism, pathological gambling, binge eating, and attention-deficit disorder," may all be linked to a genetic defect that causes low dopamine levels in the brain. Other "defects" may be responsible for everything from homosexuality to depression and panic disorders. And lately, we've been told that the brains of some criminals may be different from normal brains. What if an abusive childhood or early head trauma scrambled the hardwired brain configurations of certain individuals and turned them into helpless automatons predestined to commit violence against their fellow human beings? Is it fair to hold these damaged individuals responsible for their behavior?

Richard Dooling, *George*, February 1998.

The cell bodies of serotonin-producing neurons are located in the midbrain, from where they extend their fibers to the cerebral cortex, making about half a million connections with higher centers that deal with emotions and decision making. These fibers interact with at least 16 different types of receptors in the higher centers. Most evidence suggests that the receptor for serotonin known as 5-HT-1B is most important in modulating violent behavior. More recent evidence indicates that the 5-HT-1A receptor may also be involved. Just as the therapies for illnesses such as Parkinson's disease, Huntington's disease, Alzheimer's disease, schizophrenia, and depression have improved by manipulating the levels of certain brain chemicals, the treatment of episodic dyscontrol may be improved by manipulating serotonin levels or pharmacologically stimulating the 5-HT-1B receptors.

Norepinephrine (noradrenaline) is another neurotransmitter involved in violent behavior. This chemical seems to be out of balance in certain individuals, but its role is different from that of serotonin. It helps turn on the autonomic responses that accompany high emotions, such as increases in heart rate, respiration, perspiration, and so forth. When the brain perceives a threat, norepinephrine turns up the body's engines to prepare it to cope with the impending crises.

Norepinephrine levels are high in certain violence-prone individuals. A gene responsible for monoamine oxidase A, an enzyme that breaks down norepinephrine, seems to be defective in a single Dutch family line in which norepinephrine levels are high. The disorder, which affects only men, manifests itself as mild retardation and sudden outbursts of violence, including rape, arson, and attempted murder. Drugs that decrease norepinephrine levels tend to decrease aggressive behavior without dulling one's intellect or consciousness. Norepinephrine and serotonin may work in concert to regulate aggressive behavior.

Genetics and Violence

While others have searched for the causes of violence in TV programming, some neuroscientists have focused on the genetic programming of rodents. Researchers have developed several genetically engineered violent mice that have either low levels of serotonin or fewer serotonin receptor sites. French neuroscientist René Hen developed one such mouse, the "outlaw mouse," whose gene for the 5-HT-1B receptor was deleted. It attacks intruders with remarkable ferocity.

One study of violent Finnish criminals demonstrated an association between altered serotonin levels and a possible flaw in a gene for tryptophan hydroxylase, an enzyme important for the synthesis of serotonin.

People can inherit defective genes that make them more likely to have a low level of serotonin, but early life experiences also have a role in determining how that gene will be expressed. It appears that stressful or traumatic childhood experiences can lead to the full expression of these genes. Violence, poverty, neglect, harsh discipline, or sensory deprivation may influence the brain's serotonin production, making children with defective genes more prone to violent behavior. A healthy, stimulating environment seems to minimize the expression of these defective genes and the resultant violent behavior.

Episodic dyscontrol is more common in men than in women, but in the case of women, violence is often related to the premenstrual syndrome. Over 60 percent of violent crimes committed by women occur in the premenstrual week. The anomaly in which a male may have one X and two Y chromosomes has also been credited with predisposing him toward violent behavior.

Alcohol and certain drugs can also block the ability of our cerebral cortex to inhibit the violent tendencies of our lower brains. They produce a temporary condition rather than a chronic one. Not only is this effect of alcohol greater in people who have low serotonin levels, but alcohol itself tends to lower serotonin levels. Individuals who have taken certain street drugs, such as PCP (phencyclidine) often exhibit explosive behavior. . . .

Helping the Violent

We now know that the brain can malfunction because of conditions over which a person has no control, and that this malfunction can lead to impulsive violent behavior. This close relationship between neurologic dysfunction and violent behavior calls for more participation by neurologists in the assessment and treatment of these patients. Most people engage in violent behavior because of the situation they are in. Some do it because they are sick, and those are the people who require clinical help.

> "*Scientists in general cannot yet say that a specific abnormality in the brain causes a person to exhibit a particular violent behavior.*"

The Role of Brain Damage in Causing Violence Is Overemphasized

Bettyann H. Kevles and Daniel J. Kevles

Brain abnormalities are not a primary cause of violence, Bettyann H. Kevles and Daniel J. Kevles assert in the following viewpoint. They claim that biological explanations for violence have a long and troubling history and argue that humans do not act solely on the basis of biological signals. In addition, the Kevleses contend that theories linking brain damage to violence can have troubling repercussions, such as laws that would stigmatize certain individuals. Bettyann H. Kevles is a science writer and Daniel J. Kevles is a professor of humanities at the California Institute of Technology.

As you read, consider the following questions:
1. According to the authors, how many pages of the National Research Council's assessment of violent research were devoted to biological explanations?
2. What trait did mid–nineteenth century phrenologists claim led to violence, as explained by the Kevleses?
3. According to the authors, what gene did a California hospital link to behaviors such as drug abuse, gambling, and alcoholism?

Excerpted from Bettyann H. Kevles and Daniel J. Kevles, "Scapegoat Biology," *Discovery*, October 1997. Copyright © Bettyann H. and Daniel J. Kevles. Reprinted with permission from *Discovery* Magazine.

B iological explanations of violence are much in vogue. Part of the reason is that scientists studying the seat of behavior, the brain, and its genetic underpinnings, have learned a lot in recent years. Tendencies toward violence, they tell us, may reside in our genes or be hard-wired into our brains. Some neuroscientists have mapped brain abnormalities in laboratory animals and human murderers that seem to correlate with aggressive behavior. Others have teased out apparent connections between violent behavior and brain chemistry.

Being scientists, these researchers often try to tone down and qualify the connection between violence and biology. But even a faint message seems to fall on extraordinarily receptive ears. The findings of a team of Dutch and American scientists, for example, were exaggerated not only by the lay media but by the technical press as well. The researchers had come across a Dutch family in which, for five generations, the men had been unusually prone to aggressive outbursts, rape, and arson. These men were also found to have a genetic defect that made them deficient in an enzyme that regulates levels of the neurotransmitter serotonin. Han Brunner, a geneticist at University Hospital in Nijmegen, the Netherlands, and a member of the team, cautioned that the results concerned only one family and could not be generalized to the population at large, but the caveat was ignored. Stories everywhere, in both the scientific journals and the general media, spoke of his finding an "aggression gene."

There are other examples. In a 464-page assessment of the state of violence research in 1992, the National Research Council devoted only 14 pages to biological explanations. Of those 14, genetics occupied less than two pages. All the same, the *New York Times* covered the report with the headline STUDY CITES ROLE OF BIOLOGICAL AND GENETIC FACTORS IN VIOLENCE. Indeed, the proliferation of genetic explanations for violence prompted a *Time* writer to note wryly: "Crime thus joins homosexuality, smoking, divorce, schizophrenia, alcoholism, shyness, political liberalism, intelligence, religiosity, cancer, and blue eyes among the many aspects of human life for which it is claimed that biology is destiny."

A Fascination with Violence

Editors, of course, usually know what's on the minds of their audience: from rapes and murders in Rwanda or Bosnia to wrong-turn drivers cut down in a Los Angeles cul-de-sac, senseless violence has seemingly become the norm. Theater and movie audiences in the 1950s were shocked by *The Bad Seed*, the tale of a prepubescent pigtailed blond girl who was revealed to be a multiple killer. Today Americans are numb to nightly news reports of assaults in once-protected middle-class neighborhoods, child and spousal abuse in outwardly respectable homes, and clean-cut teenagers or even young children killing each other. The American Academy of Pediatrics made violence the theme of its meetings in October 1996, and the American Medical Association has alerted us to the "epidemic of violence."

This morbid fascination is to some extent justified: violence is pervasive. Homicide is the second leading cause of death among teenagers and young adults and the leading cause among African American women and men between the ages of 15 and 34. In the past few decades, the demographics of violence in the United States have taken a turn for the worse. Almost 80 percent of murders used to involve people who knew each other. That figure has fallen to less than 50 percent. These statistics suggest that your chances of being wiped out by someone you've never met, and probably for no reason at all, have risen.

The escalation in random violence, especially among adolescents, has generated a hunger for explanations. Biological accounts of murderous behavior do as well as any, and better than most. They are easy to grasp in principle, and they are socially convenient, locating criminal tendencies in our natures, about which we can currently do little beyond incarcerating the wrongdoers, rather than in nurture, which we might be able to remedy if we chose to invest the time and money.

The History of Biological Theories

The long, embarrassing history of biological theories of violence suggests caution. In the mid–nineteenth century, phrenologists—who diagnosed personality traits by the location of bumps on the head—worked out a behavioral map of the human skull, determining that area number 6 (out of 35) was the seat of destructiveness. In the early twentieth century some biologists and psychologists sought to extend the newly minted science of genetics to explanations of pernicious behavioral traits. Like today's scientists, they worked in a context of mounting social problems, including the disruptions of industrial capitalism and the flooding of immigrants into the nation's cities. They convinced themselves that poverty, alcoholism, prostitution, and criminality leading to violence all arose, in the main, from a trait called feeblemindedness, an inherited condition that they claimed was transmitted from one generation to the next as regularly and surely as the color of hair or eyes. Henry Goddard, the leading authority on the subject in the United States, taught that the feebleminded were a form of undeveloped humanity, "a vigorous animal organism of low intellect but strong physique—the wild man of today."

Genes Do Not Determine Behavior

Brains and minds aren't Swiss Army knives equipped with pull-out screwdrivers and bottle-opener modules, pre-formed in our genes; they develop dynamically and coherently as part of the constant interplay of specificity and plasticity that constitutes the living processes that create us. Neither behaviours, nor any other aspect of living systems, are embedded in individual "selfish genes."

Steven Rose, *Independent*, January 19, 1998.

Perhaps not surprisingly, Goddard's theories were suffused with the bigotry of his era. Feeblemindedness was held to occur with disproportionately high frequency among lower-income and minority groups—notably recent immigrants from eastern and southern Europe. The biologist Charles Davenport, director of the Carnegie Institution Station for Experimental Evolution in Cold Spring Harbor, New York, and one of the country's prominent eugenicists, predicted that the "great influx of blood from Southeastern Europe" would rapidly make the American population "darker in pigmentation, smaller in stature, more mercurial . . . more given to crimes of larceny, kidnapping, assault, murder, rape, and sex-immorality."

Such explanations of violence were commonplace in their day, but of course they proved to be hogwash, of no greater merit than the phrenological theories that had preceded them. The scientists responsible for them generally ignored the role of environment in shaping human behavior. They neglected to consider that the genetic contribution to aggression might well be very limited and, to the degree it might exist, very complex, the product of multiple genes acting in concert.

All the same, blaming violence on biology never lost its appeal to the media, the public, and even some scientists. In the mid-1960s a team of British researchers reported that a disproportionate number of male inmates in a Scottish hospital for patients with "dangerous, violent, or criminal propensities" had an extra Y chromosome accompanying the normal male complement of one X and one Y. Eventually, further research showed the double Y to be irrelevant to violent behavior, but not before lawyers representing the notorious Chicago multiple murderer Richard Speck announced that they planned to appeal his case on the grounds that he was XYY and therefore not responsible for his criminal acts. As it turned out, Speck didn't have the double Y chromosome after all, but the publicity helped inspire others to take up the banner. *Time* and *Newsweek* spotlighted the alleged relationship between chromosomes and crime, and a series of novels such as *The XYY Man* and *The Mosley Receipt* by Kenneth Royce featured an XYY character who struggled against his compulsion to cause havoc.

Today's biological theories of violence are far more sophisticated than their forebears. Unlike the earlier theories, they are concerned with behavior in individuals rather than groups, and they tend to be sensitive to the role of environment. They are also the product of some of the most powerful tools of modern science, including the ability to identify and isolate individual genes and to obtain pictures of the living brain. Unlike the phrenologists, neurobiologists can see—and show us—what may be wrong in a criminal's head.

Examining the Brain

Brain scans in particular seem to give a dramatic view into the biological dynamics of violence. Early PET-scan studies in the 1980s revealed that the brains of convicted criminals who had been victims of child abuse had areas of inactivity relative to the brains of control subjects (probably the result of getting banged on the head while they were babies). By early 1997, a psychologist at the University of Texas Medical Branch in Galveston could conjure up red-and-blue reconstructions of the brains of violent offenders and use them to support his view that their hair-trigger tempers were the result of an impairment of the frontal and parietal lobes of their brains.

Neuroscientists have isolated and begun to study the roles of several neurotransmitters in suicidal patients, depressives, and people prone to impulsive violence. They have connected both excesses and insufficiencies of serotonin and dopamine with impulsive violent behavior and with diseases of the brain such as Parkinson's. At the same time, the mapping of the human genome is providing pictorial representations of where our genes reside in relation to one another. We can now see our genes as strings of beads, and it seems only a matter of time before the bad bead on the string will be correlated with the suspect area in the brain scan. . . .

Both scientists and popularizers have predicted that the new behavioral genetics will lead to the kinds of therapies and cures that medical genetics hopes to achieve for physical disease. Yet for all its sophistication and, in some cases, caution and care, the new biology of violence is at risk for many of the difficulties that have afflicted the entire field of human behavioral biology since the early decades of this century. Researchers continue to find it difficult to eliminate or compensate for environmental influences in their studies. For instance, putting together a control group of families that have the same complicated situations as a subject group is an inexact process, to say the least. Controlling for the existence of, say, poverty is relatively straightforward, but controlling for a family's attitude toward its own poverty—and attitude will have a big impact on how well family members cope with it—is practically impossible.

Problems with Biological Theories

Many theories also suffer from imprecise definitions of the traits they purport to explain, or they lump disparate behaviors together—such as putting all manifestations of violence under the catchall category of "aggressiveness." These call to mind Charles Davenport's efforts to find genetic explanations for "nomadism," "shiftlessness," and "thalassophilia"— a love of the sea that he discerned in (male) naval officers and concluded must be a sex-linked recessive trait. Contemporary scientists have attributed to genes the propensity to crave thrills, to have leadership qualities, to be unhappy, to divorce, and to wear a lot of rings (or "beringedness," as one psychiatrist calls it). Researchers from City of Hope, the Duarte, California, research hospital, declared that the D_2 dopamine receptor gene was associated with an entire constellation of destructive behaviors, including autism, drug abuse, attention-deficit hyperactivity, post-traumatic stress disorder, pathological gambling, Tourette's syndrome, and alcoholism.

The new biology of violence has often drawn excellent correlations from studies with animals, particularly mice and monkeys. But what animals have to tell us about human behavior is severely limited. It is difficult to see how the sex lives of adolescent mice, for instance, has much at all to do with our sons and daughters. When a male rodent mounts a female, and the female assumes an accepting position, they are not doing so as a result of social pressures: both animals are acting according to biological signals alone. It doesn't take a Ph.D. to know that such is not the case with boys and girls. Monkeys, on the other hand, are certainly behaviorally closer to humans. After all, they undergo many of the same developmental stages, and anyone who has watched adolescent vervets knows that they sometimes act a lot like college students the week after exams. But monkeys are not people by any measure.

Despite all that neuroscientists have learned about brain chemistry and structure, they in fact still know very little about how the brain works, let alone how it governs action. Much confusion over research on the biology of violence occurs because the public does not always appreciate the largely correlational aspect of the research. Scientists in general cannot yet say that a specific abnormality in the brain causes a person to exhibit a particular violent behavior; they can say only that the two tend to occur in the same individual. Although in some cases an abnormality may indeed be said to cause a behavior, it is sometimes equally plausible that a behavior causes an abnormality. Further muddying the waters is the obvious and unenlightening fact that all behavior—even learned behavior—is in some sense biological. We initiate a biological process every time we use a finger to press a button or pull a trigger. The biological activity that scientists observe can often be the result of our experience in life or even "pre-life" in the uterine environment. Researchers are still a long way from predicting, much less preventing, most outbursts of violence.

How Society Might Respond

Meanwhile, even the hope of using biology to foretell an individual's tendency to violence poses grave difficulties for a democratic society. The prospect strikes directly at conventional notions of human dignity and freedom. If we could tell that someone has a 65 percent chance of behaving violently if he consumes alcohol, how should that information be used? Should it be made public, thus stigmatizing the person? Should legislation be passed making it illegal for such people to drink? Since the advent of the XYY research, many have worried that screening children for biological propensities to violence could lead to a self-fulfilling prophecy. Telling children that they are prone to violence might just encourage them to meet those expectations.

Another difficulty arises from the not unreasonable notion that if biology is destiny, then responsibility becomes moot—a point not lost on defense lawyers. In 1982, John Hinckley, who shot Ronald Reagan and James Brady, was sent to a mental hospital instead of prison in part because a jury accepted CT scan evidence that he was suffering from "shrunken brain" and had therefore not been responsible for his actions. While brain scans have not been used successfully to exculpate murderers, they have been employed to avoid the death penalty, and in the last several years criminal defense lawyers have proposed that a deficiency in the enzyme that regulates serotonin might make a good legal defense.

We would probably all like to cure society of violent behavior with something akin to a vaccine to prevent its spread and an antibiotic to cure what we already face. But the medical analogy gives undue weight to the biological basis of the behavior. "We know what causes violence in our society: poverty, discrimination, the failure of our educational system," says Paul Billings, a clinical geneticist at Stanford. "It's not the genes that cause violence in our society. It's our social system." We need better education, nutrition, and intervention in dysfunctional homes and in the lives of abused children, perhaps to the point of removing them from the control of their incompetent parents. But such responses would be expensive and socially controversial. That we are searching, instead, for easy answers in the laboratory is a sign of the times.

"Certain social factors are risk markers of higher rates of violence and battering."

Male Violence Against Women Has a Variety of Causes

Richard J. Gelles

Many factors lead to male violence against women, Richard J. Gelles contends in the following viewpoint. According to Gelles, these factors include low self-esteem, a quest for power and control over the female partner, and stress. He asserts that these factors indicate that male violence is not equally distributed among all social classes and groups. Gelles is the Joanne T. and Raymond B. Welsh Chair of Child Welfare and Family Violence, School of Social Work, at the University of Pennsylvania in Philadelphia.

As you read, consider the following questions:
1. According to studies cited by the author, what personality disorders are common among men who assault intimate partners?
2. According to Gelles, what age group is most likely to commit battery?
3. What type of drinker is most likely to batter, as stated by the author?

Excerpted from Richard J. Gelles, "Male Offenders: Our Understanding from the Data," in *What Causes Men's Violence Against Women*, edited by Michèle Harway and James M. O'Neil. Copyright © 1999 Sage Publications, Inc. Reprinted with permission from Richard J. Gelles.

This [viewpoint] reviews the data on risk factors or correlates of men's violence against women. There has been some heated debate regarding what the risk and protective factors are for men's violence toward women. Some spokespersons argue that violence cuts across all social groups, whereas others agree that it cuts across social groups, but not evenly. Some researchers and practitioners place more emphasis on psychological factors, whereas others locate the key risk factors among social factors. Still a third group places the greatest emphasis on cultural factors; for example, the patriarchal social organization of societies. In addition, . . . the source of data has an effect on the factors and variables that are identified as risk and protective factors. When basing an analysis of risk and protective factors on clinical data or official report data, risk and protective factors are confounded with factors such as labeling bias or agency or clinical setting catchment area. Researchers have long noted that certain individuals and families are more likely to be correctly and incorrectly labeled as offenders or victims of family violence. Similarly, some individuals and families are insulated from being correctly or incorrectly labeled or identified as offenders or victims. Social survey data are not immune to confounding problems either, because social or demographic factors may be related to willingness to participate in a self-report survey and tendency toward providing socially desirable responses.

The final caveat is that any listing of risk and protective factors may unintentionally convey or reinforce a notion of single-factor explanations for family violence. Clearly, no phenomenon as complex as domestic violence could possibly be explained with a single-factor model. Equally clear is the fact that almost all of the risk and protective factors discussed in this [viewpoint] and in the literature have relatively modest correlations with domestic violence. This [viewpoint] reviews risk factors for heuristic purposes, with the full knowledge that multiple factors are related to domestic violence and that there is often an interaction between and among risk and protective factors.

Drawing from research on child abuse, studies of violence against women have examined whether batterers were themselves victims of battering when they were children. The results of studies using various data collection techniques consistently find that batterers are more likely to have been abused when they were children than are men who were not abused. Although the magnitude of the association varies from study to study, nearly all examinations of batterers find some association.

More important than being a victim of violence as a child is *witnessing* violence between parents. Men who witness their fathers hit and batter their mothers are more likely to batter as adults than are men who have not witnessed violence toward women.

Mike Luckovich. Reprinted with permission from Creators Syndicate.

On occasion, some investigators and observers place too much emphasis on these findings and transform a probabilistic relationship into a single factor or deterministic explanation. Although the association between experiencing and witnessing violence during childhood and later exhibiting battering behavior tends to be consistent and strong, it is neither the only nor even the most important factor that explains or predicts battering. When the inter-generational transmission of violence occurs, it is probably the result of a complex set of social and psychological processes and is confounded with other risk markers, such as marital conflict and socioeconomic status.

A number of individual characteristics are associated with battering. Batterers tend to have a significantly lower self-esteem than nonbatterers. Batterers are significantly more depressed than nonbatterers. Investigators, however, caution that low self-esteem and depression may not be directly causally related to battering. Self-esteem may lead to battering or arise as a result of the battered women leaving the relationship. Similarly, depressive symptoms may arise after the abusive behavior. Because most of the studies that examine self-esteem and depression among batterers are clinical studies or entail the collection of data from men in treatment programs, it is at least plausible that lowered self-esteem and depression arise concurrently with or after the battering incident and are not precursors to violence. Most researchers, however, believe that low self-esteem *is* a precursor to battering.

A number of studies have found a high incidence of psychopathology and personality disorders—most frequently antisocial personality disorder, borderline personality organization, and post-traumatic stress disorder—among men who assault intimate partners. Batterers appear to be a heterogeneous group, which has led some researchers to develop typologies to represent different subgroups.

Power and Control

There is a constellation of individual and relationship factors that supports the notion that battering arises out of men's need and desire to use power and coercive control with their partners. A number of researchers have found strong relationships among status inconsistency, status incompatibility, and battering. Men whose educational attainment, occupational attainment, and income are less than those of their partners (status incompatibility) are more likely to batter. Similarly, men whose occupational attainment or income is lower than would be expected due to their educational attainment (status inconsistency) are also more likely to batter. Thus, men who fail to attain the culturally expected dominant position in the family are more likely to use verbal, physical, and sexual abuse to achieve control in the absence of material and cultural sources of power and dominance.

More individually focused research on batterers finds that batterers tend to show less assertiveness toward their wives than nonabusive men. Abusive men are "less assertive in expressing their wants and needs in a socially appropriate and growth oriented manner". Deficits of assertiveness or verbal expressiveness and insufficient problem-solving skills might provoke violence as a way to handle conflicts and difficulties.

Research points out that batterers have difficulties with "developing close, intimate relationships, based on mutuality." For some men, intimacy is threatening and reinforces their dependency on their wives, thus leading to an increased use of verbal and physical force.

A review of 52 case comparison studies did not find significant differences in measures of sex-role inequality between violent and nonviolent couples. In a later analysis, the authors observe that expectations about division of labor in the household were one of the four markers associated with a risk factor they labeled *marital conflict*—the other three markers were marital conflict, frequency of husband's drinking, and educational incompatibility.

Social Factors

A commonly held belief in the field of family violence in general, and woman battering in particular, is that violence and abuse cut across all social classes and groups and that anyone can be an abuser. Although there is indeed much empirical support for this conventional wisdom, the data consistently indicate that although abusive behavior cuts across social groups and categories, it *does not do so evenly*. Certain social factors are risk markers of higher rates of violence and battering.

Age As with all forms of violence and violent criminal behavior, battering is more likely to be committed by men under 30 years of age.

Employment Unemployed men have higher rates of battering than employed men. Blue-collar workers report higher rates of battering than workers with white-collar occupations.

Income Given the data on employment and occupation, it

is no surprise that men with a low income or who reside in low-income households have higher rates of abusive behavior toward women.

Stress and Marital Conflict The mechanism through which unemployment, low income, and other factors seem to work to produce battering is likely to be stress. The greater the number of individual, familial, and social stressors individuals encounter, the greater the likelihood of battering behavior. [Gerald T.] Straus and his colleagues (1980) found a direct relationship between stress and battering only for those men between the poverty line and the highest-income group. It seems that those in the top-income group can use economic resources to insulate themselves from the stress of stressor events. For those below the poverty line, the effects of poverty may be so pervasive that additional stressors have little important effect on the likelihood of violent behavior.

[Murray A.] Hotaling and [David] Sugarman's (1990) meta-analysis of factors related to male violent offenses found that high levels of marital conflict and low socioeconomic status emerged as the primary predictors of an increased likelihood and severity of wife assault. However, the relationship among stressful life events, the personalities of the people affected by them, and the role of stress as a factor in marital conflict and family violence remains poorly understood. It is not clear whether violent men lack conflict management skills or whether the sources of marital conflict in seriously or frequently violent relationships are different from those that characterize relationships that are nonviolent or infrequently violent.

Social Isolation Researchers have found an association between social isolation and abusive behavior. It is not entirely clear whether the social isolation is a causal factor or a symptom of a more pervasive pattern of controlling behavior exhibited by the batterer. In other words, isolation might be a causal factor—perhaps because the lack of social networks increases the influence of stressor events—or batterers may deliberately isolate themselves and, more important, their wives or partners, as part of an overall pattern of coercive control.

Alcohol and Drugs The "demon rum" explanation for violence and abuse in the home is one of the most pervasive and widely believed explanations for all forms of violence. Addictive and illicit drugs, such as cocaine, crack, heroin, marijuana, and LSD, are also considered causal agents in child abuse, wife abuse, and other forms of abuse and violence. The relationship among alcohol, drugs, and battering is not as simple as the explanation provided in the "demon rum" mode—that alcohol and other illicit drugs reduce inhibitions and, thus, increase the likelihood of violence. [Diane H.] Coleman and Straus (1983) and [Glenda] Kaufman-Kantor and Straus (1987) found that men who drank the most did not have the highest rates of battering. Drinking frequency or drinking amount is not directly related to the likelihood of violence. The highest rates of battering were among binge drinkers. Research on drugs other than alcohol does find correlations between drug use and violence, but the causal mechanisms are much more complex than the simple "disinhibition" explanation.

"Like incarcerated men, criminal women tend to have troubled and violent backgrounds."

Gender Has Little to Do with Female Violence

Rene Denfeld

Many theories try to explain why women commit acts of violence. According to Rene Denfeld, these theories are flawed because of their inherent biases and their artificial separation of male and female criminals. She maintains that such theories—that women are violent as a result of male influence or feminism—are inaccurate. According to Denfeld, most women who commit violence were not provoked by a man. In addition, she argues that incarcerated women are more likely to hold traditional views on gender roles, unlike feminists. Denfeld is a freelance writer based in Portland, Oregon, and the author of *Kill the Head, the Body Will Fall: A Closer Look at Women, Violence, and Aggression.*

As you read, consider the following questions:

1. According to a study cited by Denfeld, what proportion of women who killed their mates had records of violent crimes?
2. What are some of the beliefs held by incarcerated women, as stated by the author?
3. Which world leader does Denfeld believe demonstrates that conservative women are not passive?

Criminologists have long concocted elaborate, odd, and sometimes-entertaining theories on why women commit crimes.

Cesare Lombroso, an Italian physician of the mid-1800s, studied the bones of female prisoners before concluding that women criminals have a genetic predisposition to crime, evidenced by atavistic jaws and a general ape-man appearance. Sigmund Freud believed criminal women were sexually maladjusted deviants who envied male appendages.

Many criminologists have come along since to argue that women commit crimes for just about every reason possible except those that supposedly drive men, including premenstrual syndrome, faulty chromosomes, bizarre sexual inclinations, and lesbianism.

Men Are Blamed for Female Violence

It is men, however, who take the brunt of blame, whether through the seduction of an innocent, coercion, economic inequality, or abuse. An example is photographer Jane Evelyn Atwood. Writing for the October 5, 1994, *New York Times* op-ed page in an accompaniment to a remarkable series of photographs—women in prisons in the former Soviet Union, what was previously Czechoslovakia, New Delhi, and South Carolina—Atwood claimed that "most of the women I met said they had been provoked into committing serious crimes by the men in their lives."

According to Atwood, in one U.S. prison "almost half" of the women convicted of murder had killed husbands and boyfriends who had beaten them, and all of these said they had "repeatedly called for police help before resorting to homicide."

Atwood didn't say whether she checked out these women's stories. She seemed to assume they must have been telling the truth. But would we unquestioningly believe such stories coming from male convicts who had killed their wives or committed serious crimes?

Atwood didn't ask this question. She asked instead: "Are most women behind bars because of the men in their lives?"

The answer can be found in the research: probably not. Most female inmates have criminal records, just like men behind bars. According to a Bureau of Justice report, "Women in Prison," over two-thirds of female state prisoners had records. One in five had served time as a juvenile.

Arguments Against Blaming Men

Like incarcerated men, criminal women tend to have troubled and violent backgrounds. In one study of women who killed their mates, nearly a third had records of violent crimes, such as assault and weapons charges. In over half the cases, the homicide was premeditated. Quite a few women killed husbands who were asleep, passed out, bedridden, or otherwise incapacitated. The author of the study noted that "previous arrest histories suggest that some of these offenders were neither helpless nor afraid of their victims."

Some violent women may be motivated out of greed, rage, or just plain malice. Elisabeth Broderick, a wealthy divorcee who shot her ex-husband and his new wife to death in their bed, went to trial utterly unrepentant, saying the woman shouldn't have "knowingly dated a married man."

Broderick gained the support of a surprising number of sympathizers. No one claimed she was abused. She was bitter her alimony was "only" sixteen thousand dollars a month.

It seems dubious to me that the more than eighteen thousand women who are arrested for motor vehicle theft each year are stealing cars to escape from abusive husbands. Or that women murder their children because their husbands "provoked" them. The explanation that women act violently only when forced into it by men remains popular, but it seldom works when applied to actual people, practices, and incidents.

Interviewing female terrorists for her book *Shoot the Women First*, journalist Eileen MacDonald discovered women have been instrumental in many terrorist movements and groups, from the Palestinian Intifada to the Irish Republican Army. They are also sometimes directly involved in violence, including murder, bombings, and kidnappings. These women chafe considerably at the suggestion their acts are a result of coercion or blind love, taking such questions as insults to their passion for the cause.

Some feminists blame men for female crime—and some conservatives blame feminism. The idea that equality is creating a new female criminal was popularized by criminologist Freda Adler in the 1970s. Adler wrote that as "women are no longer indentured to the kitchens," they "are forcing their way into the world of major crimes."

Women today do have opportunities that cloistered women of the past didn't have. Yet that doesn't mean that feminism causes crime. The women's movement has largely been in response to economic changes outside its control. If organized feminism had never happened, women today would still have to work.

Given ample opportunity, most men and women will not break taboos against acts such as murder. When people do break these taboos, as the Susan Smith case illustrates, a traditional lifestyle doesn't stop them.

A key problem with blaming feminism for crime is the assumption that women criminals are more "liberated" in their views than most women. Studies show that women in prison tend to hold traditional beliefs. Contrary to their own actions, incarcerated women will say that women should be submissive, faithful to their husbands, and not drink, smoke, or break the law. In fact, both male and female prisoners tend to hold more ultraconservative values than the general population.

I find the fact that so many incarcerated women hold traditional views completely fascinating. If so many women who commit violence hold conventional beliefs, why do we continue to believe aggression is "unnatural" in women?

Some Female Aggression Is Acceptable

I believe a certain amount of female aggression is condoned, especially when it is posited as protecting children or the community. It was women, for instance, who spearheaded opposition to school integration and busing.

In *Warriors Don't Cry*, a memoir of one of the nine black students who integrated Little Rock Central High in 1957, Melba Pattillo Beals writes of being chased, kicked, and beaten by mobs of angry white women as she tried to attend her new school. The mobs continued their vigilance for months, and even the schoolteachers watched indifferently as the students—male and female—physically and verbally assaulted the black children.

Characteristics of Adult Women on Probation, in Jail, and in Prison

Characteristics of women	Probation	Local jails	State prisons	Federal prisons
Race/Hispanic origin				
White	62%	36%	33%	29%
Black	27	44	48	35
Hispanic	10	15	15	32
Other	1	5	4	4
Age				
24 or younger	20%	21%	12%	9%
25–34	39	46	43	35
35–44	30	27	34	32
45–54	10	5	9	18
55 or older	1	1	2	6
Median age	32 years	31 years	33 years	36 years
Marital status				
Married	26%	15%	17%	29%
Widowed	2	4	6	6
Separated	10	13	10	21
Divorced	20	20	20	10
Never married	42	48	47	34
Education				
8th grade or less	5%	12%	7%	8%
Some high school	35	33	37	19
High school graduate/GED	39	39	39	44
Some college or more	21	16	17	29

U.S. Department of Justice, December 1999.

Beals writes of one incident when her class was out in the exercise yard and three adult women protesters jumped the fence to attack her: " 'Nigger . . . nigger . . . ,' one woman cried, hot on my heels. 'Get the nigger.'. . . I was running at top speed when someone stuck out a foot and tripped me. I fell face forward, cutting my knee and elbow. Several girls moved closer, and for an instant I hoped they were drawing near to extend a hand and ask me if I needed help. 'The nigger is down,' one shouted. 'She's bleeding. What do you know. Niggers bleed red blood. Let's kick the nigger.' . . . As I scrambled to my feet, I looked back to see the brigade of attacking mothers within striking distance, shouting about how they weren't going to have me in school with their kids."

It was Beals's schoolmate Elizabeth Eckford who was immortalized in a photograph shown around the world. She stood there clutching her schoolbooks while surrounded by a horde of screaming, hateful women.

But because much female aggression is cast as a misguided but fundamentally well-intentioned protectionism, or as an understandable reaction to circumstances outside our control, we don't give it the same potency as male aggression. It is rarely recognized as a proactive effort designed to fulfill selfish needs; an exercise in brutality cloaked in the myth of the maternal instinct. Because of this, the most violent women can maintain women are the naturally gentler sex, and all of society will agree.

The traditional views of many violent women pose provocative questions. Will the final convincing demonstration of women's aggression be found not among those who champion equality, but, instead, among women political leaders who express violence when supporting conservative issues of family and patriotism? The feminist gains that traditionalist women might disavow have allowed them positions of power, and from podiums and political office such women may break remaining stereotypes of female passivity. You'd be hard-pressed to find a more conservative woman than Margaret Thatcher, who as prime minister led Great Britain into the war in the Falklands.

However, I don't believe the release of middle-class women from the kitchen will significantly increase violent crimes by women, any more than it will increase violent crimes by men. Breakthroughs in the glass ceiling do not drive crime. Crime tends to follow trends—from economic depressions to sentencing—that have nothing to do with women's rights. After all, the percentage of spousal murders committed by women was much the same in 1958 as it is today.

Difficulty Finding the Causes

Those who blame men for female crime and those who blame feminism have more in common than they think. Both associate crime and delinquency with gender. Both assume that the female criminal is more masculine than other women, either because she is forced to be or because she wants to be.

But crime is not the provenance only of men, and crime is not necessarily masculine in intent, success, or failure. In the Bureau of Justice study on female prisoners, for instance, almost half the women said they were drunk or high on drugs when they committed the crime that landed them in jail. Like male prisoners, many reported daily drug abuse.

It's impossible to unravel these factors from socialization and biases, to know precisely what causes female crime and what inhibits it. This information gets lost in the artificial separation of the female criminal from the male.

| *"We need to face the fact that we are an exceptionally violent nation."*

American Culture Leads to Violence

E.J. Dionne Jr.

In the following viewpoint, syndicated columnist E.J. Dionne Jr. asserts that the combination of permissive gun laws and a violent-prone culture are what ultimately lead to shootings in cities such as Fort Worth, Texas, and Littleton, Colorado. Dionne argues that America is far more violent than other developed countries, in part because of this nation's frontier spirit. He asserts that reasonable gun laws are needed to end mass killings.

As you read, consider the following questions:

1. In the author's view, which two types of culture might be linked?
2. How does Franklin Zimring explain the difference between violence and lethal violence, as quoted by Dionne?
3. Why does Dionne find George W. Bush's comments on the Fort Worth shooting irrelevant?

C an't we now ask: Isn't there something powerfully troubling about this year [1999] of mass killings, one after
another after another?

The seven people killed in Fort Worth were shot dead in
a church by a deranged man shouting anti-religious epithets.
Might that not move us to a touch of reverence before we
descend into our "it's guns/it's the culture" shouting
matches? Reverence in this case is defined not as saccharine
expressions of empathy for the dead and the wounded but as
a willingness to contemplate what might be wrong with us.

America Is a Violent Nation

We need to face the fact that we are an exceptionally violent
nation. There is no developed country like ours when it
comes to killing.

But we don't like to think that of ourselves. Each time one
of these horrible things happens—at Columbine High
School and in Atlanta and in Arkansas and in Los Angeles—
many perfectly sensible things are said: that someone quite
mad or troubled is behind the latest horror; that individuals
are accountable for what they do and their responsibility
should not be diluted by blaming society; that our talk-
crazed media culture is too eager to draw big lessons from
isolated acts.

All true, but also an evasion. "This mania is unknown in
any country in the world," Father Robert Drinan, law professor and former congressman, said on CNN. Again, you
could say many other countries have had deadly shooting
sprees. Other places—Russia and South Africa come to
mind—have bigger crime problems. You might reasonably
urge that we not get hysterical, since we are finally having
some success in bringing crime under control. But Drinan is
still right: There is a lethal combination in our country of a
violence-prone culture and gun laws that are more permissive than in any comparable nation. There is no getting
around either fact.

If we're honest, we'll ask if there might be a link between
the culture of weaponry and the culture of movie and television violence—two different forms of glorification of the
very aggression we claim to despise. And we might acknowl-

edge that the frontier spirit we revere as part of our history and culture may have a dysfunctional side when it comes to shaping our current lives in cities and suburbs.

American Crime Is Especially Lethal

We also need to make distinctions between ordinary crime and lethal acts, as Franklin Zimring and Gordon Hawkins pointed out in an important article [in 1997] in the journal *The Responsive Community*.

"What sets the United States apart from other countries is not our high crime rates," they wrote. "What sets the United States apart is our distinctively high rates of lethal violence. Our cities have no more property crime than major cities abroad. . . . But the rate of violent death from assault in the United States is from 4 to 18 times as high as in other G7 [Group of Seven] nations; and this is largely a consequence of the widespread use of handguns in assaults and robberies."

The Government Encourages Violence

The government, on all levels, teaches us that violence is "good" when you dislike someone enough. The government executes people because they have offended us. We go to war because our egos/prides are stubbed.

The government justifies and rationalizes the violence it imposes upon its victims. Citizens learn from that example that violence is "good" if it can be justified or rationalized.

Edgar St. George, "Our Culture of Violence," www.prisoners.com/violcult.html.

In an interview, Zimring, a law professor at the University of California at Berkeley, colorfully explained the distinction between violence and violence leading to death. "You're just as likely to get punched in the mouth in a bar in Sydney [Australia] as in a bar in Los Angeles. But you're 20 times as likely to be killed in Los Angeles."

Zimring rightly cites these facts as an argument for tougher gun laws. But he's too honest an analyst to pretend that gun laws explain everything. Americans, he says, are also more likely to kill people with knives than citizens of comparable countries. There is something in our culture, he says, that makes us "much more likely to consider it legitimate as part of getting into a fight to use means that threaten deadly results."

So, yes, we're back to guns and the culture. Is it possible this time that the president and his political opponents in Congress might recess the usual argument and encourage an objective look—fat chance, I know—at the causes of violence and a bit of national soul-searching leading to action?

"I don't know of a law—a government law—that will put love in people's hearts," Gov. George W. Bush of Texas said in response to the Fort Worth slaughter. Of course that's right—and utterly irrelevant. You don't have to love someone not to shoot them. We don't ask politicians to make us love each other. We ask them to criticize attitudes and ideas that lead to more killing and to pass reasonable laws that will make killing less likely.

*"Adequate consideration of urban violence
should take into account the processes of
discrimination begun many years ago."*

Racial Discrimination and Inequality Cause Urban Violence

Joan McCord

In the following viewpoint, Joan McCord argues that violence in urban America is the result of a history of unequal treatment of and discrimination toward minorities. She contends that blacks have been refused economic opportunities since the nineteenth century. McCord maintains that the effect of such inequality is resentment and anger. She claims that the actual target of such anger are wealthy and powerful people who treat the poor as undeserving, but that the ultimate victims are those close by, which is why urban violence is most commonly committed by and against black Americans. McCord is a professor of criminal justice at Temple University in Philadelphia.

As you read, consider the following questions:

1. What type of jobs were blacks excluded from after the Civil War, according to McCord?
2. According to Albert K. Cohen, as cited by the author, what is the primary goal of delinquency?
3. In McCord's opinion, what must be done in order to rebuild a civil society?

[Nineteenth-century writer] Alexis de Tocqueville argued persuasively that American culture is permeated both by a rhetoric of equality and by a strong emphasis on personal success. He suggested the result was a disquieting emphasis on symbols of status presumed to be available to all. Tocqueville postulated that when

> the distinctions of ranks are obliterated and privileges are destroyed, when hereditary property is subdivided and education and freedom are widely diffused, the desire of acquiring the comforts of the world haunts the imagination of the poor, and the dread of losing them that of the rich.

Francis Joseph Grund, an immigrant from Vienna around 1827, reported that American society

> is characterized by a spirit of exclusiveness and persecution unknown in any other country. Its gradations not being regulated according to rank and titles, selfishness and conceit are its principal elements; and its arbitrary distinctions the more offensive, as they principally refer to fortune.

Robert E. Park similarly observed, "The tenets of American democracy had done away with the aristocratic titles that ranked people in Europe. But in this professedly egalitarian society the modern city accepted a hierarchy in which money was the badge of distinction." E. Digby Baltzell, analyzing a failure of the American educational system to engender commitment to public service among the upper class, attributed it to "a society which, ideologically and morally, places such an emphasis on material success".

Success and Equality

A presumption of equality, underlies the belief that anyone can be successful. Being successful is, on this assumption, a sign of character and the proper basis for self-esteem and privilege. What counts as success will differ, of course, in relation to where one is in a social hierarchy and what one considers as justified expectations.

Tocqueville and Gunnar Myrdal were among the many reporters on America who deplored the unequal treatment of blacks and American Indians. "The Negro helped to make America what it was and what it is," noted Benjamin Quarles, a historian trying to correct the silence about contributions blacks have made to what is right in America. When the Civil War began, there were 488,070 free blacks. In Chicago, where a small pocket of free blacks had formed a community, "the laws of the state forbade intermarriage and voting by Negroes. Segregation on common carriers and in the schools and theaters was widespread". In Philadelphia between 1838 and 1860, while occupational opportunities for whites were increasing, "blacks were not only denied access to new jobs in the expanding factory system . . . they also lost their traditional predominance in many skilled and unskilled occupations." Even after the Civil War, blacks were largely excluded from educational institutions and factory as well as white collar occupations.

There is another factor to be considered when attempting to understand violence—and that is the appearance of injustice. During the 1960s, the civil rights movement promised a better world, a world in which blacks would be given the opportunities so long denied them. That promise brought with it a new sense of injustice when discrimination continued.

Discrimination Can Lead to Violence

The key to understanding high rates of violence may lie, as suggested by [Theodore] Hershberg, in comprehending the urban context of discrimination and structural inequality facing black residents of American cities in a country promising equality for all. [Robert] Sampson found that "the worst urban contexts in which whites reside with respect to poverty and family disruption are considerably better off than the *mean* levels for black communities." [Loïc] Wacquant and [William J.] Wilson suggested that

> the cumulative structural entrapment and forcible socioeconomic marginalization resulting from the historically evolving interplay of class, racial, and gender domination, together with sea changes in the organization of American capitalism and failed urban and social policies . . . explain the plight of today's ghetto blacks.

"It is not equality of *condition* but equality of *opportunity* that Americans have celebrated," wrote Stephan Thernstrom. He continued, "If careers are genuinely open to the talented, if all have an equal chance to compete for wealth, power, and prestige, the distribution that results is deemed just, however unequal." Democracy as practiced in America, however, has not made opportunities equally available to all. Nevertheless, because American culture has its roots in commitment to equality, differences in wealth or power give rise to moral tensions. The rich have reason to believe they are deserving. Those who are powerful tend to believe they earned their status and that their social status marks them as superior.

One result of moralizing differences in wealth is that the rich tend to treat the poor as undeserving. In doing so, they contribute to resentment among the poor. Resentment, rather than jealousy, seems to motivate some of the destruction accompanying modern urban riots, what seems to be pointless violence, and a good deal of juvenile delinquency.

The Causes of Urban Violence

At first consideration, perception of injustice may appear to have little to do with current urban violence because blacks so frequently are targets as well as perpetrators. Yet targets of violence often are not the source of anger. An angry person may hit the wall as a substitute for his opponent. A frustrated worker may kick the cat. Targets of anger may be hard to reach, but targets of aggression must be proximate. Although wealthy and powerful people are primary targets for this type of 'justified" anger, segregation tends to make them unavailable as targets for aggression.

Albert K. Cohen described the dominant type of delinquency that arose from subcultures as *"non-utilitarian, malicious* and *negativistic."* He identified the process by which youngsters become delinquents as one in which a boy learns that he is not to be included in activities that more affluent and powerful peers make attractive. Cohen concluded, "It seems reasonable to assume that out of all this there arise feelings of inferiority and perhaps resentment and hostility."

Cohen considered improved status, a characteristic that depends on group responses, to be the primary goal for delinquency. More recently, the theory has been transformed to suggest that a desire for improved self-esteem (which can be seen as a product of having a certain status) motivates delinquency. Although attempts to show that delinquency results from desires to improve self-esteem have a mixed history, the descriptive value of Cohen's work, particularly in the light of analyses of ghetto black culture, remains important.

In his interviews with violent men, Hans Toch provided numerous examples of the types of perceived challenges that generate assaultive behavior, those situations that engendered resentment in the assailants. For example, quoting a male convict who had responded to a question about whether his victim had encouraged an assault, Toch wrote, "'He laughed, you know, he laughed. This righteously did make me angry cause he's more, or less trying to floor show for the young ladies he's with.'"

The History of American Homicide

I believe it is clear that "the United States is a high-violence environment," that it is indeed a violent society. The high U.S. homicide rates have a historical background: the genocide of the Indian population, the institution of slavery, the widespread racism directed at American Indians, African Americans, Hispanic Americans and other minorities, and the increasing militarization of the country's economy, ideology, and governmental policy. These are major factors, though undoubtedly not the only ones, that account for our high homicide rates. Serious action to combat racism, poverty, and militarism must be at the core of the public health program to reduce violence. To borrow Alonso Salazar's final sentence in *Born to Die in Medellín:* "If we cannot do this, all that will happen will be more crocodile tears, shed whenever the United States is shaken by yet another inevitable spate of killings."

Milton Terris, *Journal of Public Health Policy*, vol. 19, no. 3, 1998.

Jack Katz identified three features of typical homicides: self-righteousness, lack of premeditation, and the absence of a clear connection between the assailant's goals and the results of his actions. One of the problems an assailant addresses, argued Katz, is to "transform what he initially senses as an eternally humiliating situation into a rage. In rage, the killer can blind himself to his future, forging a momentary sense of eternal unity with the Good." Among the cases he reviewed, Katz also found that, in "virtually all robberies, the offender discovers, fantasizes or manufactures *an angle of moral superiority* over the intended victim."

High rates of societal violence seem partially explicable as reflections of an emphasis on presumed equality in the face of a reality that is exclusionary, coupled with concern for status differentiations and a learned tolerance for the use of violence. The long-term impact of racial inequality on black self-esteem and blacks' attitudes toward laws, John Davis suggested, produced the "bitterness turned inward" represented by high levels of violent crime committed by blacks against black. One consequence of this violence has been the tendency among whites to justify discriminatory practices. The absence of historical perspective encourages misunderstanding. Whereas racial discrimination contributed materially to criminalization of blacks who were "as fully ready as any group of urban newcomers to participate in the new industrial economy from which it was barred . . . the criminality created by racism has been used over time to justify racism, as the former black skills have become dissipated."

Inner-city residents have little faith that their interests are protected by those who hold power in America. Recognizing the high degree of racial discrimination that continues, Herbert J. Gans argued that "racial minorities in the underclass will not be helped economically until white Americans become less fearful and hostile." Among other suggestions, Gans proposed using pluralistic polling to increase political representation of the varied perspectives of the urban poor. Some adjustments will be necessary in order to increase the benefits inner-city residents receive from the larger society or else they will not perceive that society as one with which they have a social contract.

Government Needs to Be Fair

Unless the governed perceive justice in the activities of government, they will have a difficult time believing in the legitimacy of its laws. As noted many years ago by Thomas Hobbes, ownership of property requires governing laws. Otherwise, physical possession amounts to ownership and there can be no such thing as theft. Without some degree of faith in legal protection, self-protection appears to be the only option. Private "justice" operates where there are no legitimate authorities. "Where there is no common Power, there is no Law: where no Law, no Injustice," wrote Hobbes. Government requires, at a minimum, an exchange of benefits—be they merely protection or more complicated rights. A democracy requires more.

Adequate consideration of urban violence should take into account the processes of discrimination begun many years ago. These processes trapped blacks in cities that were themselves disadvantaged by government policies that supported development of suburbs and the migration of jobs away from cities. The policies that encouraged industrial migration stripped cities of a reasonable financial base and left many residents with little hope for better times to come.

Political rhetoric continues to emphasize equality of opportunities, and mass media have democratized expectations for the material benefits available from success. At least some of the poor know they are not being given the opportunities that have been promised. Rage comes easily. The history of unjust distribution of opportunities may well have undermined commitment to a social contract. If so, programs aimed simply at adjusting individuals to the present social system will not be sufficient. Redesign of the social contract may prove necessary in order to rebuild a civil society.

> "People who are stoned, high, and wasted
> are likely to commit crimes of all kinds,
> including violent crimes."

Drug Use Leads to Violence

Robert L. DuPont

In the following viewpoint, Robert L. DuPont contends that drug use often leads to violence. He argues that the self-centered and hedonistic values that are the basis of crime are the same as those that lead to drug use. DuPont asserts that another way in which drug use results in violent crime is by impairing the brain. According to DuPont, because drugs have a detrimental effect on the brain, drug legalization would likely worsen the crime problem by making drugs more available. DuPont is the president of the Institute for Behavior and Health in Rockville, Maryland.

As you read, consider the following questions:

1. What does DuPont believe led to the escalation in crime in Washington, D.C., during the late 1960s?
2. According to the author, why have many people responded positively to the idea of drug legalization?
3. In DuPont's opinion, what approach is most effective in ending a drug addiction?

Excerpted from Robert L. DuPont, "Violence and Drugs," *Journal of Psychoactive Drugs*, October–December 1997. Reprinted with permission from the author.

For me the issue of drugs and violence triggers an intense and personal review of the experience of the last 30 years with these contentious and vital problems, and most of all the questions of how they are related to each other and what can be done to substantially reduce both violence and drug use. In 1967, after completing a psychiatric residency at Harvard and as I was finishing my two-year stint in the U.S. Public Health Service Commissioned Corps (an alternative to military service during the Vietnam War), I looked for my first job outside of medical training. Inspired by the lives of my two heroes, John F. Kennedy and Martin Luther King, Jr., I turned to the goal of reducing serious crime which was then just becoming epidemic. I saw the best opportunity in the application of public health principles, working directly with convicted criminals. Giving a medical twist to the adage of the time, attributed to bank robber Willie Sutton, who, when asked why he robbed banks, responded simply "Because that's where the money is," I reasoned that it I could do something to help those folks with the worst criminal records, I could help not only them, but also their families and their communities. To achieve this goal, I went to work full-time at the District of Columbia Department of Corrections, setting up an office in Lorton, Virginia, in one of the nation's most notorious prison complexes.

Although my initial ideas focused on community-based alternatives to incarceration (which necessitated high-intensity care in the model of the therapeutic community) I was quickly convinced that the rapid rise in heroin addiction was one of the root causes of the escalation in crime in the nation's capital. I looked for ways to reduce the rates of heroin use in the community, working with the heaviest users of heroin, convicted felons who were released to the community on parole and probation. Using the multimodality treatment approach pioneered in Chicago by Jerome H. Jaffe, M.D., with a major emphasis on methadone maintenance, I started the first corrections-based comprehensive addiction treatment program in 1969, while I served as head of the city's parole program.

On February 18, 1970, the mayor of Washington, D.C., asked me to extend my work beyond corrections to establish a city-wide treatment system in the District of Columbia. Thus was born the Narcotics Treatment Administration (NTA). By the middle of 1973, NTA had treated more than 15,000 heroin addicts from 20 treatment centers located in all parts of the city with a staff of more than 400. At that point I was chosen by President Nixon to succeed the distinguished Dr. Jaffe as the country's second White House Drug Czar, and to start the National Institute on Drug Abuse (NIDA), where I served as the first director from 1973 to 1978. While many considered this a promotion, I had a great feeling of loss leaving corrections and my original goal and, equally troubling, leaving direct patient care at the community level for the rarefied bureaucratic air of the federal government.

The Problems of Addiction and Crime

As the 1990s draw to a close, the United States continues to grapple with the twin scourges of addiction and crime. The search for viable solutions is as urgent today as it was 30 years ago. The expenditures now being made in both criminal justice and the prevention and treatment of addiction are staggeringly large compared to the expenditures in the late 1960s. They exceed even the most aggressive plans of that era. Despite these efforts, the problems of drugs and crime remain huge, although most people would now describe them as "endemic" rather than "epidemic" since they have become chronic and apparently intractable.

There are those who would "solve" the drug problem by legalization of prohibited drugs, a solution that makes as much sense as solving the problem of bank robberies by legalizing that prohibited behavior. But the siren call of legalization finds a responsive chord in many people in all parts of America today precisely because of the failure of the good ideas of the past three decades to solve the problems of drugs and crime.

Even the linkage of drug use and crime remains fraught with controversy as many people believe that the connection is no more than coincidental. While the historically important Drug Use Forecasting Data (DUF) pioneered by Eric Wish, Ph.D., has given us the best evidence of the high correlation of illegal drug use and crime, the doubters can point to an equally high correlation of crime and cigarette smoking, saying, "You don't claim that cigarette smoking causes crime even though a larger percentage of incarcerated felons smoke cigarettes than the general population. How can you claim that heroin or cocaine use, much less alcohol or marijuana use, causes crime?"

The Connections Between Drug Use and Violence

At the heart of this controversial connection of crime and drugs is the concern not about all crime or even about all serious crime, but about violence (including assault, robbery, rape, and murder), the most frightening manifestation of criminal behavior. While some are filled with doubt about the connection of alcohol and other drug use and violence, I have a different perspective based on 30 years of working with individual criminals. It is clear to me that the desire to get money for prohibited drugs is only one of many ways that drugs cause crime.

Marijuana Use Can Lead to Violence

Marijuana, which pro-legalizers consider harmless, may have a connection with violence and crime. [Barry] Spunt and his colleagues attempted to determine the role of marijuana in the crimes of the homicide offenders they interviewed in the New York State prisons. One-third of those who had ever used marijuana had smoked the drug in the 24-hour period prior to the homicide. Moreover, 31 percent of those who considered themselves to be "high" at the time of committing murder felt that the homicide and marijuana were related. William Blount of the University of South Florida interviewed abused women in prisons and shelters for battered women located throughout Florida. He and his colleagues found that 24 percent of those who killed their abusers were marijuana users while only 8 percent of those who did not kill their abusers smoked marijuana.

James A. Inciardi and Christine A. Saum, *Public Interest*, Spring 1996.

The most important ways that alcohol and other drug use are related to violence are these: first, the self-centered, impulsive, and hedonistic values that underpin crime also underlie the use of illicit drugs. Values matter a lot in human behavior and they matter especially in both crime and drug use. When people get well from both crime and addiction, they develop new values that place concern for others and delayed gratification, to say nothing of religion, on far higher levels of importance than when they were pursuing, deadly careers as criminals and drug addicts. Second, alcohol and other addictive drugs (not including nicotine) cause the users' brains to work poorly. The intoxicated brain is an impaired and a "selfish brain." This intoxicated impairment quite literally leads people to commit impulsive, destructive crimes, including crimes of violence.

People who are stoned, high, and wasted are likely to commit crimes of all kinds, including violent crimes such as assault, robbery, rape, and murder. Intoxicated people are also more likely to cause accidents and to be the victims of accidents, including motor vehicle accidents, than are people whose brains are working without the impairing effects of alcohol and other drugs. Alcohol use is a major cause of violence, although alcohol is so cheap that even the poorest people can get it without committing income-generating crimes. The connection of alcohol use and violence should give the would-be legalizers cause for second thoughts.

Why Legalization Will Not Reduce Crime

If the major way drug use was linked to crime, including violence, was the high cost of prohibited drugs, then some form of harm reduction or legalization to make heroin, cocaine, marijuana, LSD, and other prohibited drugs available might make sense as a crime reduction strategy. However, since making drugs more available and cheaper would inevitably lead to greater levels of use, it follows that if the major way drug use is linked to violence is through the impairing effects of this use on brain functioning, this approach would make the problems of crime (including violence) worse. That, put simply and directly, is my belief: the major way alcohol and other drug use causes violence is through altered brain functioning. Therefore, making drugs more available would worsen the problem of violence in our communities. Greater drug availability would make the lives of both the perpetrators and the victims of violence worse. It would also worsen the corrosive fear of crime, which is a major negative effect of crime in modern America.

When it comes to getting well from addiction, the best, the most reliable and the most effective path is through active participation in the 12-Step programs, including Alcoholics Anonymous and Narcotics Anonymous (DuPont & McGovern 1994). A few years ago, I had one sentence quoted on network TV news summarizing my work as the White House Drug Czar. My one line was, "The 12-Step, programs are the secret weapons in the war against drugs." People often complain about the media shortchanging them. I had, in this case, the opposite feeling. In that short quote I had a simple and powerful summary of all that I had learned in the past 30 years of dealing with the closely linked problems of drug abuse and crime.

My dream of helping to solve the crime problem is alive and well, as is my conviction that reducing the use of nonmedical drugs is the single most powerful strategy available to cut the rate of crimes, including violent crime.

Periodical Bibliography

The following articles have been selected to supplement the diverse views presented in this chapter. Addresses are provided for periodicals not indexed in the *Readers' Guide to Periodical Literature*, the *Alternative Press Index*, the *Social Sciences Index*, or the *Index to Legal Periodicals and Books*.

Fox Butterfield	"A Fatality, Parental Violence, and Youth Sports," *The New York Times*, July 11, 2000.
Richard Dooling	"The Evil Mind," *George*, February 1998. Available from 1633 Broadway, 41st Floor, New York, NY 10019.
Neil S. Jacobson and John Mordechai Gottman	"Anatomy of a Violent Relationship," *Psychology Today*, March/April 1998.
David Kirby	"What's in a Basher's Mind?" *Advocate*, September 28, 1999.
Brendan Lemon	"The State of Hate," *Advocate*, April 13, 1999.
Philip LoPiccolo	"Something Snapped," *Technology Review*, October 1996.
Ralph Peters	"The Future of War," *Maclean's*, April 26, 1999.
Mark Pilisuk and Jennifer Tennant	"The Hidden Structure of Violence," *ReVision*, Fall 1997. Available from Heldref Publications, 1319 18th St. NW, Washington, DC 20036-1802.
Aysan Sev'er	"Recent or Imminent Separation and Intimate Violence Against Women," *Violence Against Women*, December 1997. Available from Sage Publications, 2455 Teller Rd., Thousand Oaks, CA 91320.
Kathy Sitarski	"The Wheel of Violence," *Humanist*, May/June 1996.
Thomas Szasz	"Does Insanity 'Cause' Crime?" *Ideas on Liberty*, March 2000. Available from the Foundation for Economic Education, Irvington-on-Hudson, NY 10533.
Milton Terris	"Violence in a Violent Society," *Journal of Public Health Policy*, vol. 19, no. 3, 1998. Available from 208 Meadowood Dr., South Burlington, VT 05403.
Nicole Walker	"Why Women Are Committing More Crimes," *Jet*, July 3, 2000.

CHAPTER 3

What Factors Lead to Youth Violence?

Chapter Preface

For many people, the term "youth violence" is commonly associated with school shootings or robberies and murders committed by young gang members. However, youth violence can also include sexual assaults and other forms of violence against women. On June 11, 2000, more than two dozen men reportedly groped, stripped, and robbed as many as sixty women in New York City's Central Park. Although a few of the suspects were men in their thirties, the majority of those arrested were young men in their teens and early twenties. Many questions have been raised in the wake of this incident, perhaps most importantly, why it occurred in the first place.

Los Angeles Times staff writer Alisa Valdes-Rodriguez argues that the attacks on the women were caused at least in part by misogynistic song lyrics. She writes: "The idiots who ripped the clothes off the women in Central Park were *raised* on gangsta rap and aggro-rock. It did not *reflect* their world view, it *formed* it." Valdes-Rodriguez also observes that the attacks in Central Park were just one in a series of recent events, such as those that occurred at the 1999 Woodstock Festival, in which popular rap and rock lyrics were chanted by assailants during their attacks.

Not everyone believes popular music should be blamed for youth violence, however. Although he wrote the following words prior to the Central Park attacks, Danny Goldberg, the copublisher of *Tikkun* magazine, represents the views of those who maintain that pop music is not the insidious influence that many believe. Goldberg observes: "Youth-oriented entertainment criticized as harmful turns out on closer inspection to be, at worst, innocuous. In popular music, . . . the most popular albums [in 1999] were by Britney Spears and the Backstreet Boys."

The influence of popular culture is just one explanation that has been offered for youth violence. In the following chapter, the authors consider whether this and other factors lead to youth violence.

"*Higher levels of viewing violence in the mass media are correlated with increased aggressive behavior.*"

Violence in the Media Can Lead to Youth Violence

Elizabeth K. Carll

In the following viewpoint, Elizabeth K. Carll asserts that exposure at an early age to media violence is a factor in violent behavior among youngsters. She contends that music videos, movies, television programs, and video games include excessive amounts of violence, which can lead to children and adolescents accepting aggressive attitudes. Carll maintains that explicit images of sexual violence in movies, which causes desensitization toward violence against women, is a particularly serious effect of media violence. Carll is a psychologist whose interests include interpersonal, family, and workplace violence.

As you read, consider the following questions:

1. According to a study cited by the author, by the end of their teenage years, children have seen how many violent acts on television?
2. In Carll's view, what is the effect of films that show women willingly being raped?
3. What is the "copycat" phenomenon, as defined by the author?

Excerpted from Elizabeth K. Carll, *Violence in Our Lives*. Copyright © 1999 Allyn & Bacon. Reprinted/adapted by permission.

Violence as entertainment is evident in everyday media ranging from film, TV, radio, print, music videos, and theater, as on the New York stage in Paul Simon's musical "The Capeman." This $11 million production is about a notorious teenage killer who fatally stabbed two Hell's Kitchen youths in 1959. The highly publicized murders resulted in years of media attention with the press branding the killer, Salvador Agron, age eighteen, as "The Capeman." Agron's death sentence was later commuted, and he was released from prison in 1979. Seven years later he died of natural causes.

According to a news report the play, which previewed at the end of 1997 and opened the beginning of 1998 sparked considerable controversy, with threats of boycotts and lawsuits. Parents of Murdered Children, a victim's family group, and Murder Is Not Entertainment, a watchdog group, protested the show. The controversy ignited articles as well as a cartoon captioned "It all started with 'Capeman'" appearing in the *Daily News*. Battered by angry protests, scathing reviews, as well as production problems, the show closed several months later. However, plans were under way to develop national and international touring productions and a possible concert tour featuring the show's music.

The Effects of Music Videos and Video Games

Many children and adolescents watch music videos. A study of music videos found that both males and females who were rated higher in their acceptance of rape myths and stereotypes were more likely to attribute more responsibility to the women for forced sex. Obviously, the media continue to perpetuate these rape myths, which in turn serve to perpetuate acceptance of rape. In certain situations, they may actually be fueling the wave of violence against women. Note also that there is serious concern not only about the content of the media's portrayal of violence but also about the increased airtime it receives. According to a study by the Center for Media and Public Affairs in Washington, D.C., the amount of network TV news airtime devoted to covering violent crime doubled in 1997, while the overall crime rate remained stable in the United States.

The prevalence of video games depicting repetitious murder and graphic massacre as goals of the game has also been cited as fueling the desensitization of our youth to violence. In a story about the Jonesboro, Arkansas, shooting, perpetrated by two boys ages eleven and thirteen, at a middle school resulting in the death of five and wounding of ten, the writer, Jim Dwyer makes reference to a magazine review of the new video game "Postal":

> Armed with shotguns, flame-throwers and napalm, you mow down entertainingly innocent bystanders, ranging from church congregations to high school marching bands. Your maimed and dying victims beg for mercy or run around on fire, screaming for help, every so often a woman shrieks, "He's going postal."

The callous disregard for pain and suffering and the trivialization of human life and suffering were not the basis of popular games in the past. Although these games are fantasy, they nonetheless may teach a lack of empathy for others. We need to begin to study the effects on those brought up with violent video games during childhood.

Depictions of violence in the media are not merely a contemporary phenomenon; although today's media violence is often more graphic than in the past, subtle messages were apparent. For example, in the classic 1950's sitcom *The Honeymooners*, it was not unusual for beloved comedian Jackie Gleason to raise his fist toward his wife, telling her, "Alice I'm going to send you to the moon," when she was stepping out of line or he was frustrated with her behavior. Although certainly delivered in a humorous nonmalicious tone, the line held a subtle though evident implication of the expected submissive role of women and spawned a legion of men who often said the phrase to their wives.

Increased Aggression and Emotional Harm

Naturally, much of the public has been aroused over the impact that media portrayal of violence may have on children, who may buy into the antifemale stereotypes due to the proliferation of media messages and "infotainment" (entertainment news shows).

The exposure of American children to high levels of media violence has been well documented. [A] 1992 study . . .

found that by the end of their teenage years children have witnessed over 200,000 violent acts on television. Add to this the increasing exposure to new cable channels and the use of VCRs, and the number increases even more. One popular film alone, *Die Hard 2*, contains depictions of 264 violent deaths. Moreover, the 1993 American Psychological Association's study on media violence concluded that higher levels of viewing violence in the mass media are correlated with increased aggressive behavior and increased acceptance of aggressive attitudes and that exposure at young ages can have lifelong consequences. More than a hundred such studies over the last forty years have shown that at least some children exposed to visual depictions of dramatic violence behave more aggressively afterward toward both inanimate objects and other children. These results have been found in both boys and girls of all social classes, races, ages, and levels of intelligence.

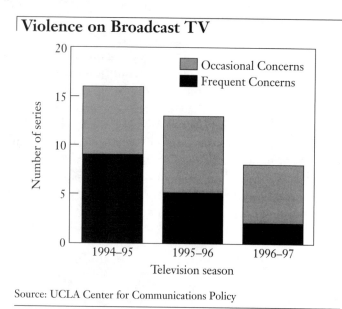

Violence on Broadcast TV

Source: UCLA Center for Communications Policy

Increased airtime for showing violence is especially noteworthy, as research with adults shows a powerful tendency for viewers to overestimate the probability of events in the real world as a function of seeing these events on television.

Thus, heavy concentrations of violence in the media tend to induce anxiety and uncertainty about future events and frequently cause sleep disturbances. Concerns from anecdotal reports about potential emotional harm induced by violent programs that depict violent events, natural disasters, and technological disasters give rise to fright, anxiety, and upset and can result in secondary traumatization.

This tendency is even greater in children (particularly between ages seven and eleven), who have only a limited understanding of the concept of probability to help them assess what they see. They have a developing recognition that such things could happen to them, but they also naturally have far less experience with the real world. A survey of five hundred children eight to twelve years old by *USA Today* and Nickelodeon Channel concluded that almost two-thirds of children reported having been scared or upset by violence on news shows or reality-based programs.

Violence Against Women

Consider what reports of rape and violence teach young girls, ages seven to eleven, some about to enter puberty. What kinds of impressions will develop concerning male–female relationships? Research and anecdotal reports suggest that the media's portrayal of violence and women may have a significant impact on the perceptions of men, women, and children and in the long run affect the health and well-being of our society. Studies have shown that explicit depictions of sexual violence (as in R-rated films) and graphic news stories about violence against women appear to affect the attitudes of male youths about rape and violence toward women.

The 1992 report on televised violence by the APA Task Force on Television and Society, as well as other recent research into media violence, considered the implications of exposure to sexually violent materials due to increasing opportunities for such exposure through R-rated cable and/or VCR viewing. Sexual violence in the media includes explicit sexualized violence against women, including rape and images of torture, murder, and mutilation. Films that depict women as willingly being raped have been shown to increase men's beliefs that women desire rape and deserve sexual abuse. Male youths who view sexualized violence or depictions of rape on television or in film are more likely to display callousness toward female victims of violence, especially rape.

Younger viewers often lack the critical viewing skills to discount myths about women and sexual violence, and these myths may have a deleterious influence on developing attitudes toward sexuality. A male youth's first exposure to sex may be in the form of an erotic but also violent movie, such as a slasher film, not uncommon in video movies. Thus, early attitudes are formed linking sex and violence that may be carried into adulthood. We are experiencing an epidemic in youth violence and most likely will continue to see even more desensitization to sexual violence.

The Copycat Effect

One of the most obvious effects of media violence is the "copycat" violence phenomenon, in which there is a direct imitation or copying of violent or antisocial behavior. While many cases of copycat teen suicides have been documented, and there has been at least some attempt to minimize media coverage in this type of case, the same has not been true with regard to sexual violence or aggression toward women. Within a week after the murder of Nicole Simpson, a young woman in New York was gang raped, slashed forty times, and murdered. Two days later, following that report, a young woman was stabbed repeatedly and pushed from a moving car by a male companion on their first date, also in New York. Other parts of the country had similar experiences. Coincidence, or a contagious effect? New York certainly has its share of violence, but usually it involves guns; now, suddenly, the weapon of choice was a knife, wielded against a woman.

The news media claim to report reality. Rare but horrifying accounts, however, have appeared in which the reality was created for the sake of the media, for instance, in the production of underground "snuff" films, porno movies which culminate in the actual murder and dismemberment of an actress. The *New York Post* (October 1, 1975) carried a story about a nationwide investigation into snuff films, which were usually shot in South America and circulated on the "pornography connoisseur circuit," where select clientele could afford $1,500 for a collection of eight reels. As an example of the powerful contagious and copycat effect of the media, four months after the *Post* story ran, a porno movie called *SNUFF* opened at a first-run movie theater on Broadway in New York City, advertised as the "bloodiest thing ever filmed." More recently, allegations of a snuff film's being made were reported on an August 1994 edition of the television newsmagazine *Hard Copy.*

It can be concluded, then, that viewing media violence has three basic detrimental effects:

1. Learning aggressive and violent behavior
2. Becoming desensitized to violence and suffering
3. Becoming fearful of being victimized, including developing an increased distrust of others sometimes described as the "mean world syndrome"

> "If the media was at fault, . . . everyone of the some 1,850 students at Columbine would all be killers."

Violence in the Media Should Not Be Blamed for Youth Violence

Jack Valenti

Media violence should be not blamed for youth violence, argues Jack Valenti in the following viewpoint. He contends most adolescents are exposed to the same movies and television shows but only a few of those teenagers become violent. Valenti acknowledges that there are unacceptable movies, but he asserts that most filmmakers recognize the role they play in society and the responsibility they have to make parents aware of films that are inappropriate for children. Valenti is the president and chief executive of the Motion Picture Association of America. The viewpoint is excerpted from testimony he gave before the Senate Commerce Committee.

As you read, consider the following questions:
1. According to statistics cited by Valenti, what percentage of schools reported a serious violent crime in 1996?
2. What does the author think should be the responsibility of creative teams?
3. Why does Valenti think American society needs to listen to children?

Reprinted from Jack Valenti, testimony before the Senate Commerce Committee, May 4, 1999.

114

What happened at Columbine High School in Colorado was a senseless act of mindless malice. Every sane American recoils in horror. There is rage in the land. There are outcries to ban, abolish, and quarantine by legislative fiat what many believe to be source beds of fatal mischief. But we have to be clear-headed in our response to the query: How does this nation make our schools proof against such grotesque intrusions? . . .

Youth Violence Is Decreasing

One doesn't have to be a medical seer to understand that youngsters who kill, wantonly, casually, are inhabited by dismal rhythms which dance in an emotional bubble perilously off-center. There is within them a mental disconnect swarming with dark and primitive transactions. Unhappily, no one knew that behind the fresh faces of Eric Harris and Dylan Klebold lurked the picture of Dorian Gray. Why did not anyone sense that these two seemingly non-violent youths were seething with hatred, on the edge of detonation, even though it was writ clear and large they were in terrible emotional disarray?

But when something incomprehensible like Columbine occurs, fear is infectious. In a *Newsweek* poll [in April 1999,] 64% of adults believed a shooting incident at their local schools to be "very likely" to "somewhat likely." But factually in 1996 only ten percent of schools reported even one serious violent crime.

The statistics are revelatory. Fewer than one percent of homicides involving school-age children occur in and around schools, according to the Centers for Disease Control. Since 1992 the annual death toll from school shootings has ranged from twenty to fifty-five, says the National School Safety Center. There were forty-nine deaths in the [1997–98 school year]. Forty-three percent of all schools had no crime at all in the 1996–1997 school year, said the Department of Education. In 1997, 8% of high school students said they had carried a weapon to school in the preceding month. This was a decrease from the 12% in 1993.

In 1997, the murder rate in the USA was the lowest in thirty years. The juvenile violent arrest rate rose between 1988 and 1994, but peaked in 1994, and since then has decreased steadily. The FBI reports that the number of persons under eighteen in the U.S. is some 70 million. The rate of arrests for violent crimes in this category has declined from its high water mark in 1994 at .51% to .41% or forty-one hundredth of one percent (287,000). This also means that 99.59% of young people under eighteen (69.7 million) were not into violent crime.

The children of this country do not deserve being all herded into a category that labels them as something they are not. They are not all killers. They are not all brooding, menacing figures, filled with hatreds, emotional abnormalities which house a defective mythology. Though all children more or less inhabit the same entertainment and community enclaves, ninety-nine percent of them are decently formed good citizens.

Yes, I know that statistics are frail reeds on which to lean, but they ought not be ignored. Yes, it is absolutely true that one death is too many. Columbine happened. The nation weeps. Now we have an overpowering responsibility, as a nation, to make our schools safer. . . .

The Role and Responsibility of Movies

Let's discuss movies. Accusatory fingers point toward films as a prime villain. [In 1998] the entire movie industry produced over 550 films. When that many movies are made, some of them are bound to be slovenly conceived. In a free society, no one can command "only good movies be produced." Which is why I will not defend all movies. Some few in my judgment cross a smudged, ill-illuminated line where the acceptable becomes unsuitable, and I'll have no part of them. But the great majority of films, some of them rising to the highest point to which the creative spirit can soar, don't warrant being lumped with a number of movies whose worth is questionable. Edmund Burke was right when he said, "You cannot indict an entire society." Neither should anyone condemn the many because of the porous quality of the very few. Moreover, American parents have the supreme right not to patronize what they judge to be soiling to their childrens' future. The parental bill of rights declares the power of parents to turn away from that which they don't want their family to listen to or watch. Banish them from your home, refuse to patronize them outside the home.

I do earnestly believe that the movie/TV industry has a solemn obligation. Each creative team must examine their work from a personal perspective. Is there gratuitous violence, language or sensuality? If there is, then the creative team, on its own, without any nagging or commands from anyone else, ought to exile whatever is gratuitous without dismaying the dramatic narrative that is the core of the story. I wholeheartedly endorse that kind of creative scrutiny.

The Media Do Not Cause Anger

Blaming the medication for the violence is as wrong as blaming the guns, the music or the violent video games and movies. It is not what teens hear in their music or see in the movies or video games that causes the rage. It is not the access to guns that causes their anger. Instead, it is teens' inability to handle their feelings of abandonment that causes the rage. Lacking parent and community supports, they have no one to turn to at the end of a bad day. And there are always bad days for teen-agers.

Anne Hendershott, *San Diego Union-Tribune*, June 13, 1999.

Years ago many of us in the movie world came to the conclusion that we had a duty to inform parents about film content. This is the prime reason why for over thirty years a voluntary movie rating system, created and implemented by film producers and theater owners, has been in place. These ratings give advance cautionary warnings to parents so they can decide what movies they want their children to see or not to see. Only parents are capable of making such decisions. Some 75% of parents with children under thirteen find this rating system Very Useful to Fairly Useful in helping them guide their children's movie viewing.

A comparable rating system is operative in television, offering information to parents about TV shows. Soon, there will be available in large supply the so-called V-Chip whose aim it is to give parents more power over the TV viewing of their children. Parents have to tend to their children's TV viewing, seriously, tenaciously, else they cannot indict others for their lack of monitoring TV watching in the home. For example, too many parents are agreeing to give their young children their own TV set, in their own room, thereby losing control over what their children are watching. But that is a parental decision they alone can make.

The movie industry has played, and is playing, an important role in our society, and will continue to do so. American movies travel the world, where they are hospitably received and enthusiastically patronized. Our movies, from *Mr. Smith Goes to Washington* to *Saving Private Ryan*, from *Ben Hur* to *Star Wars*, captivate audiences everywhere. Entertainment created in America is one of this nation's proudest artistic and commercial assets. We produce for this country huge amounts of surplus balance of trade at a time when the country bleeds from trade deficits. (It is ironic that Japan, which devours American films and TV programs, has one of the lowest crime rates in the world!)

We (meaning parents and citizens, Congress, White House, professionals in the field of education, science and business) should listen to the children, the youngsters in grammar school, middle school and high school. They are best equipped to tell us if the media is the complete villain, if what they hear and see infects them, and soils their best intentions. They know better than their elders about peer pressure and rejection and cliques and the mean alternatives that tantalize and entice them. Are we truly listening to them?

On Thursday, April 29, 1999, Jeff Greenfield (Cable News Network) had a "conversation" with students. Two of those students were from Columbine High School. One of them, a lovely senior named Alisha Basore, was queried about the impact of the media on unnatural behavior. She responded that the media was a minor force in distorting students' values. If the media was at fault, she said, everyone of the some 1,850 students at Columbine would all be killers because, as she pointed out, the students all watch the same movies and TV programs, listen to the same music, play the same video games. By her side was the other Columbine student, Josh Nielsen, who confirmed Alisha's remarks and said it wasn't the media, but rather that the two killers were crazy.

Let's listen to the children.

| "*Research shows that having an absent father is associated with a greater likelihood of chronic juvenile bad behavior.*"

Poor Parenting Is a Factor in Youth Violence

James Garbarino

Parental abandonment and neglect are a major reason why some boys become violent, asserts James Garbarino in the following viewpoint. He claims that these boys are less trusting and more likely to see violence as a natural response to problems. According to Garbarino, the absence of a father means a boy will lack a mentor who can steer him away from negative choices, while a boy without a mother will experience significant pain and rage. Garbarino is a psychologist and codirector of the Family Life Development Center at Cornell University in Ithaca, New York.

As you read, consider the following questions:

1. According to the author, what are some of the reasons why mothers are unable to form a secure attachment with their newborns?
2. What is the first effect of living without a father, as explained by Garbarino?
3. According to Garbarino, what was the double abandonment faced by Matt?

Excerpted from James Garbarino, Ph.D., *Lost Boys: Why Our Sons Turn Violent and How We Can Save Them*. Copyright © 1999 James Garbarino. Reprinted with permission from The Free Press, a division of Simon & Schuster, Inc.

S ome parents disappear from their child's life, psycholog- ically and/or physically. Some mothers experience what psychologists call postpartum depression during the early months of their baby's life and for a time are psychologically unavailable to their newborn, unable to form a secure at- tachment. Violence within the home, illness, extended hos- pitalization—all are factors known to impair the develop- ment of the attachment bond. Some women have strongly ambivalent feelings about being a mother, perhaps feeling they were pushed into motherhood by social or family ex- pectations when what they really wanted was to focus on their careers outside the home.

The Effects of Abandonment

Whatever the particular circumstances or barrier, social is- sues and psychological problems can prevent otherwise competent, caring individuals from succeeding in basic par- enting tasks. And when this earliest parent-child relationship doesn't take hold and thrive, a boy is left emotionally high and dry and his soul retreats deeper and deeper.

It is commonplace for the general public and politicians to attribute youth crime and violence to a breakdown of the fam- ily. In truth, the problem is not the breakdown *of* the family but the breakdown *in* the family. Disruption in the basic rela- tionships of the family figure prominently in the lives of vio- lent boys. These boys often have a strong sense of family, and they often speak about their families. In this sense, they are very big on family values. For example, Malcolm's rhetoric on family resembles that of my own Italian father in his descrip- tion of where loyalty fits into his value scheme. He says, "Nothing is more important than family, nothing. I would kill anyone to protect my family. I would die for my family, man."

But existing side by side with this feeling of family that many violent boys have is a record of the disrupted connec- tions and abandonments they have faced, often early in life. Sometimes in talking with them I get glimpses of how boys feel about these abandonments. When I ask Malcolm whom he trusts, he replies, "No one." I ask, "What about your fam- ily?" "My family," he replies, "only to a limited degree. I mean, you can't trust nobody all the way in this world."

The Importance of Fathers

To anyone who knows family life in America, it should come as no surprise that fathers play a crucial role in the development of boys. Two particular patterns of father influence are most important in understanding the development of violent boys: (1) the *presence* of an abusive father and (2) the *absence* of a caring and resourceful father. The presence of an abusive father teaches sons some very dangerous lessons about being a man, often lessons that are only unconsciously learned.

Fifteen-year-old Terrel is in jail for killing a convenience store clerk. As he talks about his history, he returns over and over again to his need to dominate people. "People are afraid of me," he says. "I like that." Terrel recounts how he assembled a group of boys who would do anything he told them to do. "I enjoyed having that power, making people do what I want. And if they disobey me, they get hurt. That's the way things are." He is currently serving a life sentence because the convenience store clerk dared to oppose him when Terrel demanded all the money in the cash register. "He said he couldn't do it," Terrel says. "So I says, 'Don't talk to me like that. Don't you ever talk to me like that.' And then I shot him."

Where did Terrel learn to be the boy he is? Having heard the story of his father's brutal treatment of Terrel and his eighteen-year-old brother, who is serving a life sentence in an adult prison, one doesn't have to took far. What Terrel describes happening between him and the convenience store clerk echoes his description of his relationship with his father: Do what I say or get hurt; submit or feel pain. When asked about this parallel, Terrel seems surprised, even stunned. "Hmm," he says after thinking it over a minute. "I never thought of it that way, but I guess you're right." Sometimes a boy is better off with no father at all than one who teaches him these lessons about manhood and violence.

Growing Up Fatherless

But boys also suffer from the absence of a caring father. Research shows that having an absent father is associated with a greater likelihood of chronic juvenile bad behavior. The link comes through at least three effects of living without a father:

First, being fatherless increases the odds that a boy will

grow up in a neighborhood where resources of all kinds are in short supply, thus, the normal opportunities for success in the world will be limited. In America today, being fatherless is one of the most powerful predictors that a child will be poor, will be moved from home to home and neighborhood to neighborhood, and will therefore have more difficulty establishing stable and positive relationships with peers. Thirteen-year-old Mitchell Johnson of Jonesboro, Arkansas, is but one example of a young boy who suffered through such instability in the years leading up to his infamous shooting spree.

Abandoned and Ignored

So what if kids are abandoned by their parents, stuck in a rundown house and forced to live unsupervised in the midst of drug-abusing, gun-selling grown-ups?

So what if they are left to feed on a daily diet of aggression and made to feel absolutely worthless?

So what if the deck is stacked against these kids virtually from birth?

That doesn't seem to faze most of us.

But should it matter only when a child gets his hands on a gun—and puts a classmate to death?

Should it matter to us only then?

Colbert I. King, *Liberal Opinion Week*, March 13, 2000.

Second, growing up fatherless increases the chances that a boy will lack a male guide, protector, and mentor. This is itself a risk factor for later delinquency, because boys in an environment with many negative possibilities require every possible counterforce to keep from succumbing to them. Having a father is no guarantee of protection (particularly if he is abusive), but it does increase the odds of success. We know that in Pearl, Mississippi, Luke Woodham fell under the influence of a particularly pernicious peer group, one that capitalized on his emotional vulnerability and drew him ever deeper into violence. Tragically, Luke's mother was unable to move him away from that group.

Finally, growing up without a father always leaves the question of why. "Why don't I have a father?" often goes unanswered. And there is always the possibility that a child will answer that question by concluding there is something wrong with him that he doesn't have a father. The repercussions from this negative conclusion pose a bigger danger for some children, particularly those with a temperamental predisposition to depression and aggression, than for others. Imagine the powerful chemical reaction when many boys who have grown up in similar circumstances, similarly hurt, get together.

Mothers Who Abandon

An absent father is one thing—and the consequences for boys of this absence are not surprising to anyone familiar with the correlation between father absence and delinquency—but what is surprising is the prevalence of absent *mothers*. Many of the boys involved in lethal violence lose their mothers for significant periods in their early years; some lose them permanently. Some have a mother in jail or in a drug treatment program. Sometimes mothers move away and leave their boys with relatives; some mothers die. The pain and rage associated with maternal abandonment is often buried deeply, but it is there nonetheless.

Matt speaks to me about his postrelease plans and says that he hopes he might be able to relocate so that he can be closer to his mother, who is herself serving a life sentence for murder at the state prison. This is the same mother who gave up caring for him when he was four and turned him over to *her* mother. Why? She wanted to protect him from his father—her pimp—who was beating and tormenting him mercilessly, and she also wanted to be rid of him because he interfered with her "lifestyle." This double abandonment may cut more deeply than the hurt other boys experience, but Matt is far from unique.

The Costs of Abandonment

British psychiatrist Michael Rutter has studied the chain reactions that are likely after a child experiences abandonment and other disruptions of early relationships. In his research it is clear that for a boy to be separated from his mother in infancy and early childhood is a very significant risk factor for future development. Rarely does one risk factor by itself tell the whole story about development, but most child psychologists recognize that early detachment is a very powerful negative influence all by itself.

In Jonesboro, neighbors report that Andrew Golden, the eleven-year-old who partnered with thirteen-year-old Mitchell Johnson to shoot down kids at their school, was raised mainly by his grandparents while his parents worked long hours. In the weeks before the shooting, his dog was lost for a time, and when it returned it was suffering from a bullet wound. For a boy whose principal activity with his father seems to have been shooting and involvement in the gun culture and who was already angry, this kind of hurt could easily have been too much to bear.

In Moses Lake, Washington, fourteen-year-old Barry Loukaitis brought an assault rifle to school a few weeks after his mother announced that she was divorcing his father and that she was suicidally depressed about this planned breakup.

Of course, none of these abandonment experiences necessarily lead to violence. Thousands of boys live with the same losses each year, yet very few take extreme measures to cope with their pain. Many become depressed and mask that depression by self-destructive behavior such as alcohol or drug addiction. And many others express it though nonlethal violence (but violence just the same). But when an abandonment experience is put in the broader context of a troubled boy's life, particularly a boy with uncontrolled access to guns, such an experience can be the spark that ignites a powder keg.

> *"Parents can't win. The impossible is
> expected of them—direction without
> discipline, monitoring and control."*

Parents Should Not Be Blamed for Youth Violence

Don Feder

In the following viewpoint, Don Feder contends that parents are wrongly blamed when their children become violent. He asserts that liberals contradict themselves by blaming the parents of juvenile mass murderers such as Dylan Klebold and Eric Harris but also by preventing those parents and other parents in similar situations from keeping tabs on their children's activities or using corporal punishment when necessary. Feder, a syndicated columnist, places the blame for youth violence on popular culture.

As you read, consider the following questions:
1. What are the contradictions in liberal child-rearing advice, in Feder's opinion?
2. According to the author, what did the United Nations Convention on the Rights of Children declare?
3. Why does Carole Collins face two and a half years in prison, according to Feder?

Reprinted from Don Feder, "Expecting the Impossible of Parents," *Jewish World Review*, May 5, 1999. Reprinted with permission from Creators Syndicate.

Except for the National Rifle Association, no one has taken more hits over the Littleton, Colorado, killings than families.

Where were the parents? critics cry. Why weren't they omniscient? The president says he'll file legislation to hold Ward and June Cleaver criminally liable when the Beav misbehaves with a gun.

Liberal child-rearing advice is a mishmash of contradictions: Monitor your child, but don't invade his privacy. Raise him to behave decently and respect the rights of others, but don't discipline him.

While they're lecturing us about our responsibilities, the elite has created a cultural sewer for adolescents to swim (or sink) in.

Pop Culture Is at Fault

The most inane observation on Littleton came from *Time* magazine contributor Amy Dickinson, who admonishes: "We must take responsibility for the world our children inhabit. We make the world for them."

Unless we are Marilyn Manson or Quentin Tarantino, I think not. We did not produce "Payback" (Mel Gibson's latest gore-fest) or "The Matrix," a film with the firepower of a NATO sortie.

We do not market videogames with names like "Doom" and "Killer Instinct," or write lyrics that exalt anarchy, sexual assault and suicide. We do not defend teens' access to Web sites that approximate the lower depths of hell.

Try to imagine a teen rampage where the killers were obsessed with the film versions of Jane Austen novels, or spent hours playing Monopoly and listening to Bach.

How could their families have raised monsters like Eric Harris and Dylan Klebold? the experts ask.

But too many children are raised by their surrogate parent—the culture.

When concerned parents try to protect youth from the more invidious aspects of the same, they're called censors and control freaks, and told their repression is apt to provoke an adolescent backlash.

The United Nations Convention on the Rights of Children, of which Clinton is much enamored, declares that children of any age have a right to freedom of expression and association, as well as a "right to privacy."

If the parents of Harris and Klebold had searched their sons' rooms for armaments and explosives, they would have violated the boys' privacy.

Chuck Asay. Reprinted with permission from Creators Syndicate.

Wearing swastikas and shouting "heil Hitler" in school was protected by the teens' freedom of expression.

Attempts to keep the kids from hanging with neo-Nazis on the Internet would have abridged their freedom of association—so say the United Nations and Bill Clinton.

For generations past, mine included, the key to successful child-rearing was moral instruction backed by stern discipline. Transgressions brought an excursion to the woodshed for a philosophical encounter with a razor strap.

Today, parents who heed the Biblical injunction about rod-sparing are likely to find themselves facing a felony rap. The Massachusetts Supreme Judicial Court will soon decide if the Rev. Donald Cobble is guilty of child abuse. [The court threw out the case in November 1999.]

When his 11-year-old son Judah is especially bad, the minister gives him a whack or two on the behind with a belt. This brought down the wrath of the state's officious child-welfare agency.

"Who are they to decide what's best for me and my family?" Cobble asks. "Of the three social workers who came and spoke to me, none were married and none had kids."

The experts counter that the minister is teaching violence at home. Why couldn't the lad have a "time out," instead. To which Cobble replies, when a policeman stops you for speeding, he gives you a ticket, not a time out ("Now, just sit in you car and quietly reflect on your violation of the traffic laws.")

In Boston, Carole Collins faces 2 and a half years in prison for giving her burly, 15-year-old son the back of her hand.

Mother and son conferred with the assistant principal of his high school to discuss discipline problems. The boy got into a shouting match with the administrator and Collins slapped her son in the face. Instead of thanking her for helping them with a fractious student, school officials called the cops and Collins was led away in handcuffs.

Parents can't win. The impossible is expected of them—direction without discipline, monitoring and control while respecting the "rights" of 12-year-olds all in the context of a culture that undermines their authority and seduces their children by playing to their darkest instincts.

Liberals—those universal Buttinskis—want to raise your children then blame you when they pack a high-powered rifle in their school bag.

> *"The teen killers' violent actions were*
> *allowed to explode by the cultural vacuum*
> *created by the absence of selfish values."*

American Culture Is a Factor in Youth Violence

Robert Tracinski

In the following viewpoint, Robert Tracinski argues that the Columbine killings occurred because the teen shooters were unaware of choices available to them beyond those offered by American culture. He maintains that Eric Harris and Dylan Klebold had been taught by American culture to believe that their only options were belief in God or life on terms dictated by their peers. Tracinski argues the teenagers, after rejecting those two options, turned to the deadly choice of nihilism—the belief that existence is meaningless—and the subsequent desire to destroy everyone as their only viable alternative. He concludes that the killings could have been avoided if Harris and Klebold had pursued personal goals rather than care about acceptance from their peer group. Tracinski is the editor of the *Intellectual Activist*.

As you read, consider the following questions:
1. Who does the right blame for the Columbine killings, according to the author?
2. In Tracinski's opinion, how were Dylan Klebold and Eric Harris "lone wolf" types?
3. According to Tracinski, how is a criminal affected by his cultural environment?

Reprinted from Robert Tracinski, "Explosions in the Cultural Vacuum," *The Intellectual Activist*, June 1999. Reprinted with permission from *The Intellectual Activist*.

On April 20 [1999], two students entered Columbine High School in Littleton, Colorado, and shot dozens of their classmates, killing 12 students and one teacher, then ending their own lives. This is the most recent—and most deadly—in a string of more than half a dozen school shootings in the past few years. These have not been shootings at inner-city schools, caused by turf wars between rival gangs. Rather, they have taken place in otherwise unthreatening rural and suburban locations, and the motive has been killing for its own sake. These shootings have touched off a nationwide scare and a number of "copycat" crimes; in the past few weeks, students across the country have been arrested for making bomb threats or carrying weapons into their schools.

The rash of shootings has also prompted a wave of articles in the press and "expert" commentary on television purporting to explain the killers' actions. Parents and school administrators are right to look for explanations. There have always been juvenile delinquents and "troubled" teens in high schools, but the two Columbine killers, Eric Harris and Dylan Klebold, were aiming for a much greater degree of mayhem: A diary found after the shootings shows that they had been planning the attack for a year and hoped to kill at least 500 people. What could prompt two young people to be so overwhelmed with hatred toward their peers that they meticulously planned a full-scale massacre?

Two False Explanations for Youth Violence

There have been two types of answers, one offered predominantly by the left, the other predominantly by the right. These explanations provide a crucial clue to the actual reason for the killings—not by what they say, but by what they leave out.

The typical explanation given by the left focuses on the children's physical and social environment. One example, an editorial by Richard Cohen in the April 22 *Washington Post*, begins by mentioning several possible psychological motivations for the killings. Cohen then dismisses them: "Pick your theory. The fact remains that we may never know what caused two kids to go berserk. We do know, though, that no matter what influenced them, they had guns." He then goes on to advocate stricter gun control. The implication is that the inner workings of the mind are a mystery not worth sorting out—"What goes on in the heads of teenagers?" Cohen asks rhetorically. Instead, we should seek to examine and control man's physical environment.

In a similar vein, a psychologist interviewed on a national news program insisted that the Columbine tragedy was a result of America's failure to institute a "national mental health system" which could have spotted the killers' "illness" and offered treatment. Again, the focus is on the physical—not the outer environment but the physical operations of the killers' glands. (Ironically, the leader of the two killers, Eric Harris, was already taking a Prozac-like antidepressant.)

But the explanation that was heard most often from the left was that these teens were driven to kill because they were "outcasts" who were rejected by their peers. Deprived of love and acceptance by others, this reasoning goes, Harris and Klebold became "loners" who were "antisocial." The May 3 issue of *US News & World Report*, which poses the question "Why?" on its cover, offers the following answer:

> William Damon, director of Stanford University's Center on Adolescence, blames the lack of community structure for pushing kids toward the odious. "Without the connectedness of real community, there's no check on the cynicism."

In other words, without social approval and group membership, no moral values are possible.

The right offers a different—and superficially more plausible—answer. The blame for the killings, in their view, rests on a culture dominated by violence, nihilism, death. They point to the rock music performer Marilyn Manson—whose pseudonym is itself an act of nihilism, blending the names of Marilyn Monroe and Charles Manson—as well as violent video games, television shows, and films. Conservative columnist John Leo, writing in the same issue of *US News & World Report*, laments the effects of gory computer games:

> We are now in a society in which the chief form of play for millions of youngsters is making large numbers of people die. Hurting and maiming others is the central fun activity in video games played so addictively by the young. . . . Can it be that all this constant training in make-believe killing has no social effects?

This question almost uncovers the proper explanation. But Leo ends there, treating video games and the like as if they are first causes, capable of no deeper explanation. He does not ask why it is that Manson is given a recording contract rather than a job at the local circus sideshow; he does not ask what causes young people to seek out mindless violence for entertainment, rather than heroic adventure stories. Instead, he views young people as being literally programmed and brainwashed by these messages. Leo quotes psychologist David Grossman: "Pilots train on flight simulators, drivers on driving simulators, and now we have our children on murder simulators."

Targeting Nihilism

Other conservatives offer similar themes, such as the claim that these killings are a reflection of the collapse of "family values," on the ground that the killers' parents must not have been spending enough time with their children. (Leo chimes in that "the primary responsibility for protecting children from dangerous games lies with their parents, many of whom like to blame the entertainment industry for their own failings.")

But most of these commentators ultimately point to the killers' nihilism as a demonstration of what happens when children are not sufficiently indoctrinated in religion and especially when prayer is removed from the public schools. Thus, the most common solution offered by the right is: more religion. If children were only given more religious instruction, the argument goes, they would have the moral guidance necessary to steer them away from acts of violence.

In epistemological terms, the left views the individual as programmed by his physical environment, while the right views him as programmed by music and television. Thus, they offer more state control of man's physical environment—or the replacement of "bad" cultural programming with "good" programming by means of school prayer and church sermons. Ayn Rand wrote (in "Censorship: Local and Express"):

> The conservatives see man as a body freely roaming the earth, building sand piles or factories—with an electronic computer inside his skull, controlled from Washington. The

liberals see man as a soul freewheeling to the farthest reaches of the universe—but wearing chains from nose to toes when he crosses the street to buy a loaf of bread.

This false alternative is precisely what is being offered in the explanations of the Columbine massacre. Either the children's brains are programmed by television, to which censorship and religious indoctrination is the only antidote—or it is impossible to discover or control what goes on in their minds, so the only alternative is to assert greater control over their bodies. Each side presents a corresponding answer in the realm of morality. The left offers, as its source of values, "connectedness" with the social group; the right offers, as its source of values, God.

The Lack of Selfish Values

Notice what is left out of these explanations: the individual. The three-way alternative is: God or the group—or nothing, i.e., nihilism. Both the left and the right deny the possibility of independent thought and of personal, *selfish* values.

Yet what is most striking about Harris and Klebold is precisely their lack of such values. The two are described as "outcasts"—but they were deliberate outcasts, who flaunted their separation from others; according to one story, for example, they once wore armbands that proclaimed, "I hate people." They were the classic "lone wolf" types, who chose not to conform to the group, but to purposely seek conflict with the group. "Whatever everyone else is," they said in effect, "I'll be the opposite." Yet to define oneself by one's opposition to the majority is still to define oneself by reference to the group.

Consistent with this "lone wolf" mentality, with defining oneself in terms of negation, the two killers were fascinated with any form of *destruction*. That is why they were obsessed with guns and violent video games and why they called their own anti-clique the Trench Coat Mafia—borrowing a name and fashion associated with killers. For the same reason, they dressed in black, listened to death-obsessed rock music, and dabbled in a fascination with Nazism. Harris's one seemingly positive act was to apply to the Marine Corps, but he did so, according to classmates, not to defend his country, but to have a legally sanctioned opportunity to kill. (It was five days after his rejection by the military that he launched his killing spree.) Class projects that the two students had completed included pointlessly violent short stories about combat and a psychology project on serial killer Jeffrey Dahmer.

An Overdependence on Mood Suppression

A ten-year-old boy, arrested after an armed stand-off with police in which he used his three-year-old niece as a human shield, entered the novel plea of 'Not Guilty due to a Prozac-induced trance.' Between the millions of kids on Prozac and the millions on Ritalin for Attention Deficit Disorder, America's schools are becoming one huge experiment in mood suppression. 'If Huck Finn or Tom Sawyer were alive today, we'd say they had ADD or a conduct disorder,' says Michael Gurian, author of *The Wonder of Boys*. 'They are who they are and we need to love them for who they are. Let's not try to rewire them.' But, for hassled parents and busy school administrators, rewiring is the easiest option. With half the students, you don't want to be around when the medication wears off; with the other half, you don't want to be around when it kicks in. But, as it's hard to tell which is which, you're best to steer clear entirely.

Mark Steyn, *Spectator*, May 30, 1998.

Perhaps the most revealing insight into the killers' motives was provided by a website created by Harris, quoted in the *Washington Post*, in which he defined his personal philosophy. After complaining about "people with their rich snobby attitude thinkin [sic] they are all high and mighty and can just come up and tell me what to do," he replies:

My belief is that if I say something, it goes. I am the law, and if you don't like it, you die. If I don't like you or I don't like what you want me to do, you die. . . . I'll just go to some downtown area in some big . . . city and blow up and shoot everything I can. Feel no remorse, no sense of shame.

Put into clearer terms, this statement says: "I am a victim . . . I am helpless, I am inferior," and then draws the conclusion: "The only way I can escape and turn the tables is by killing." This is the mark of a profound *selflessness*. It is the confession of a deep-seated feeling of inferiority and powerlessness in the face of others—bursting into a hateful resentment and a desire to gain that missing sense of power by using force.

Ironically, Harris and Klebold were complying dutifully with the perspective of the left, which tells them that the group (and one's acceptance within it) is the only source of values; and since they believed themselves to be rejected by the group, they chose destruction as their only alternative. In the same way, they were also complying with the views of the right. One of the killers is reported to have asked a victim if she believed in God. When she replied, "Yes, and you need to follow His path," he said, "There is no God"—and then shot her. Without God, these killers believed, the universe was empty and amoral, so they chose nihilism as their only alternative. In essence, they were told: In order to have morality and live peacefully with others, you must give up the self, either for God or for the group. Or: You can assert your "self" by imposing your whims through force. They chose the latter.

It is impossible to say whether the Columbine killers could have been prevented from taking some type of violent action. They were driven, ultimately, by their own choices. But as I wrote in regard to the Unabomber ("Was the Unabomber Driven by Hatred or by Ideas?" *TIA*, June 1998), a criminal's cultural environment cannot cause him to become evil, but it can give him "a direction for his hatred and a sense that he [is] acting out of legitimate personal grievance."

An Alternative to Nihilism

In this case, what encouraged these killers, what justified in their minds the wanton murder of their classmates, was the belief that there was no better alternative. The teen killers' violent actions were allowed to explode by the cultural vacuum created by the absence of selfish values.

If our children are not to become killers—or if the potential killers among them are not be unleashed—they need to discover the alternative to the deadly choices of God, society, or nihilism. They need to be taught to find their values and their moral code, not in submission to God or the group, but in personal, selfish goals. A young person with an independent mind will not care whether he is an "outcast"; he will have goals and values that are not dependent on the acceptance of the group. And a young person with a love for a productive career—someone motivated by the desire to become a scientist, or a musician, or a businessman—will not seek relief in destruction for its own sake; he will be focused on learning how to produce the values he wants to create.

But a common acceptance of the virtues of independence, productiveness, and selfishness requires a moral revolution: the overthrow of mysticism and collectivism in favor of a concept of man, in Ayn Rand's summary, "as a heroic being, with his own happiness as the moral purpose of his life, with productive achievement as his noblest activity, and reason as his only absolute." This vision, not God or society, is the only valid alternative to the nihilism underlying the motives of the Columbine killers.

"There are many . . . factors that influence the development of youth violence."

Youth Violence Has Various Causes

Ronald D. Stephens

Numerous factors contribute to youth violence, Ronald D. Stephens argues in the following viewpoint. Stephens asserts that youths that were victimized or neglected are more likely to turn to violence. In addition, he contends that the use of alcohol and drugs, involvement in a gang, and the easy availability of guns can also cause violence among juveniles. Stephens is the executive director of the National School Safety Center.

As you read, consider the following questions:
1. What percentage of bullies had previously been victimized by another person, according to statistics cited by the author?
2. How does Stephens define social skills deficit disorder?
3. In Stephens's opinion, what is the most effective strategy in preventing youth violence?

Excerpted from Ronald D. Stephens, testimony before the Congressional Subcommittee on Early Childhood, Youth, and Families, April 28, 1998.

Understanding youth violence is a complex issue which is affected by a wide variety of social, economic, political and individual factors.

In a cooperative study involving the National School Safety Center and the Centers for Disease Control, an analysis was made of "School Associated Violent Deaths" during the 1992 to 1994 school years. Specific common factors were identified among perpetrators:

- 40 percent had a past background of criminal misbehavior;
- 24 percent had been previously involved with substance abuse;
- 35 percent were involved in gangs; and
- 70 percent had previously brought a weapon to school.

Since July of 1992, the National School Safety Center has identified 211 school-associated violent deaths, most of which involved intention to cause personal injury. Using these factors and percentages, consider this:

- If 40 percent of the perpetrators had a criminal background, the inverse of this data is that 60 percent did not;
- If 35 percent were gang-involved, the inverse suggests that 65 percent were not;
- If 24 percent were drug-involved, the inverse suggests that 76 percent were not.

The data suggests that even with all we know, what we don't know is greater than what we do know. This suggests that there are many other factors that influence the development of youth violence.

Key Risk Factors

Researchers and youth-serving professionals have identified many risk factors which contribute to violence. Perhaps the top two such factors are a history of victimization and perceptions of isolation.

Past victimization. Research involving schoolyard bullies reflects that about 80 percent of bullies were first victims of bullies—in the form of parents, peers, siblings or others. Many victims become perpetrators of crime in response to their own experiences with ridicule, physical punishment, torment and abuse. The combination of being both a victim and a perpetrator makes it more difficult to understand and sort through the causes of violent behavior. The way youngsters are treated by parents is perhaps the most influential predictor of child behavior. Most psychologists agree that bullying and aggression are learned behaviors. If they are learned, the implication is that they can be unlearned.

Youngsters who feel isolated, neglected, ignored and ridiculed. This factor itself is complicated. Some suggested causes of perceptions of isolation and neglect include:

- economic deprivation that distances children and youth from peers who have advantages and comforts they lack;
- lack of growth and enrichment activities such as conversation with family members, childhood reading experiences, exposure to social activities with family members and friends, pre-school classes;
- lack of nurturing role models and persons who can serve as caring supervisors, mentors or advocates;
- youngsters' perceptions that they are not understood and not appreciated;
- conflicts and isolation perceived due to differences among the culture of the family and varieties of cultures in the school or larger community;
- family disorganization and lack of meaningful rituals (for example, shared mealtimes, birthday celebrations and family outings)

Additional Causes of Youth Violence

Other causes of violence in youth include:

A background of misconduct and trouble at home, at school and with the law. One of the best predictors of future behavior is past behavior. Youngsters who begin at home to act out, withdraw, bully others and evidence impaired attention spans reveal potential indicators of future trouble. Such children are candidates for immediate and early intervention. Consequently, prevention and early intervention activities and programs through churches, social services agencies and schools can go far to ensure that disruptive, delinquent behavior does not become ingrained.

It is critical to guide children through positive role modeling, encourage them through positive mentoring, and help them achieve success through supervision and support.

Social skills deficit disorder. A common pattern among perpetrators is a social skills deficit disorder, which is often characterized by rage, defiance, thoughtlessness, detachment and nonconnectivity. Often these youngsters feel powerless and hopeless; but with a gun, they feel powerful and in control. Several new terms have been developed over the years to describe these kinds of individuals, including, ADHD (attention deficit hyperactive disorder), ODD (oppositional defiant disorder) and IED (Intermitted Explosive Disorder).)Whatever the label, the result of disruptive, delinquent behavior is unacceptable.

School failure. School failure is a significant predictor of law offending. Because such failure is a consistent predictor or correlate of violent behavior, it may be useful to identify children who are at risk of school failure due to living in high-risk, economically deprived neighborhoods. Such children must be targeted for preschool intellectual enrichment programs, which have correlated positively with reductions among at-risk children in school failure and later offending.

Alcohol and other drugs. Use of alcohol and other drugs tends to diminish inhibitions and lower an individual's threshold for violence. School administrators across the country are looking for ways to identify early the potential for violence. For instance, Carmel High School in Indiana mandates a drug test when a youngster is suspended or expelled from school for an infraction. Early results have shown that 40 percent of students tested because of fighting tested positive for illegal substances. 42 percent of students violating the tobacco policy also tested positive for illegal substances. The good news about Carmel High's testing program is that after the testing, 64 percent of all students who tested positive for an illegal substance received treatment.

Gang involvement and gang violence. Involvement in gangs is a vicious cycle of intimidation, violence and retaliation masquerading as "belonging" and taking part in peer rituals. A sample study of 1,000 youth reported in the November/ December 1997 issue of *Juvenile Offender* reveals that adolescents who join street gangs are more involved in delinquent acts than are adolescents who are not gang-involved. Gang members were responsible for 65 percent of general delinquency, 86 percent of serious crime, 60 percent of public disorder. 70 percent of drug sales, 63 percent of alcohol abuse and 61 percent of drug use. In addition, gang members often escalate violence through their rivalries and retaliation activities. In several of the major school shootings, individuals were gang-involved or negatively influenced by peer groups. For instance, in Pearl, Mississippi, the perpetrator was a member of satanic cult; in Bethel, Alaska, and Lynneville, Tennessee, the shooters were influenced by other students.

Risk Factors for Teenagers

RISK FACTOR: Availability of firearms
- Firearms sales
- Firearms in homes

RISK FACTOR: Economic deprivation
- People, children, families living below poverty level, by race
- Unemployment
- Female family, householder with no spouse
- Free/reduced lunch program
- AFDC, food stamps

RISK FACTOR: Conflict
- Divorce
- Percentage of married people with spouse absent
- Domestic violence reports

RISK FACTOR: Rebelliousness
- Suicide rates by age
- Gang involvement
- Vandalism, graffiti reports

Developmental Research and Programs, *ABA Journal*, September 1999.

Prejudice and discrimination. Emphasis on differences, along with acts of bigotry based on differences, has perhaps done more to fuel gang membership and involvement than anything else in American society. The way others are treated, particularly newcomers, has a great deal to do with the alliances and affiliations that are formed. However, prejudice and discrimination are pervasive in society at large, not simply instrumental in encouraging the formation of gangs or other social groups. Inbred fear, hate and discrimination are often imperceptibly passed from one generation to another without any defensible justification or understanding.

Violence publicized in the media and sports. Violence is woven throughout our culture in movies, sports and the media. Our societal attraction to violence is exhibited in our crime rates and in the media. Such publicity has a significant effect on stimulating youth violence. Young people tend to become what they see and what they experience. The United States has one of the highest rates of interpersonal violence among all nations of the world. In addition, the United States has the highest homicide rate of any Western industrialized society.

Guns Are Easy to Acquire

When it comes to the media, the theme seems to be "if it bleeds, it leads." There is a tendency to showcase the most violent acts in daily news reports. Oftentimes fights at school are not reported unless there is a serious injury. Even video and arcade games have taken on a deadly and violent character. The marketing language tells the story. We've gone from "Mortal Combat" to "Mortal Combat II" to ultimate annihilation and even worse. The way we die says so much about the way we live. Death review boards across the country have observed that now when youngsters kill each other, it is often not simply a single shot that brings death to the victim, but multiple shots to the head, chest or groin, reflecting not simply violence, but raging violence.

Easy availability of guns. Despite the argument that people kill, guns don't, the easy accessibility of weapons to young people in this country is staggering.

• A 1993 study of juvenile possession of firearms drawn from questionnaire volunteer responses of 835 male serious offenders in 6 juvenile correctional facilities in 4 states and 758 male students in 10 inner-city schools near those facilities revealed:

> • 83 percent of inmates and 22 percent of the students had possessed guns;

- 55 percent of inmates carried guns all or most of the time in the year or two before being incarcerated, 12 percent of the students did so, with another 23 percent carrying guns now and then.
- When asked how they would get a gun, 45 percent of the inmates and 53 percent of the students would "borrow" one from family or friends; 54 percent of the inmates and 37 percent of the students said they would get one "off the street."

• A Harvard School of Public Health survey in 1993 revealed that of the 2,508 students surveyed (in 96 public and private elementary, middle and senior high schools, grades 6 through 12), 59 percent said that they could get a handgun if they wanted one. Two or three who knew where to get a handgun said that they could get one within a 24-hour period.

In the old days, when fistfights were the way to settle arguments, young people would walk away with a few bruises or black eyes. Today, however, with guns it is about body counts, not bruises. We have transitioned from the single shot zip guns to the six shooter to semi-automatic weapons. There seems to be a tendency to see how much more violent the next school-associated violent death can be.

Absence of responsible adult supervision. Despite all of the high-tech strategies including—camera surveillance, metal detectors, motion sensors and access control systems—still the single most effective strategy for preventing youth violence is the physical presence of a responsible adult in the immediate vicinity.

The above are just a few of the causes associated with violent juvenile behavior. We must develop recommendations for actions that parents, educators and students themselves must take to eliminate this threat to the education and development of skilled, knowledgeable, socially responsible citizens.

Periodical Bibliography

The following articles have been selected to supplement the diverse views presented in this chapter. Addresses are provided for periodicals not indexed in the *Readers' Guide to Periodical Literature*, the *Alternative Press Index*, the *Social Sciences Index*, or the *Index to Legal Periodicals and Books*.

Debra Baker — "How Safe Is Your 'Burb?" *ABA Journal*, September 1999.

Samuel Francis — "Absence of Culture Made Littleton Possible," *Conservative Chronicle*, May 12, 1999. Available from PO Box 29, Hampton, IA 50441.

Danny Goldberg — "Et Tu, Ralph Nader?" *Tikkun*, March/April 2000.

Bruce Grierson — "The Profits of Violence," *Progressive Populist*, June 1999.

Albert R. Hunt — "Teen Violence Spawned by Guns and Cultural Rot," *Wall Street Journal*, June 11, 1998.

Issues and Controversies On File — "Television Violence," February 12, 1999. Available from Facts On File News Services, 11 Penn Plaza, New York, NY 10001.

Michael Medved and David Horowitz — "Is the Problem Television or Viewers?" *American Enterprise*, March/April 1999.

Mindszenty Report — "Six Lessons from Columbine High," May 1999. Available from the Cardinal Mindszenty Foundation, 7800 Bonhomme Ave., PO Box 11321, St. Louis, MO 63105.

Peggy Noonan — "The Culture of Death," *Wall Street Journal*, April 22, 1999.

Ann Powers — "The Stresses of Youth, the Strains of Its Music," *The New York Times*, April 25, 1999.

Judith A. Reisman — "Cultivating Killers," *New American*, June 7, 1999. Available from 770 Westhill Blvd., Appleton, WI 54914.

Gary Ross — "Moving Beyond Blame," *The New York Times*, May 6, 1999.

Mark Steyn — "Virtual Violence," *Spectator*, May 30, 1998. Available from 56 Doughty St., London, England WC1N 2LL.

Tom Teepen — "Gunning for Pop Culture," *Liberal Opinion Week*, May 17, 1999. Available from PO Box 880, Vinton, IA 52349-0880.

Daphne White — "'Violence Is Not Child's Play,'" *Christian Social Action*, June 1999. Available from 100 Maryland Ave. NE, Washington, DC 20002.

CHAPTER 4

How Can Society Respond to Violence?

Chapter Preface

In 1994, Congress passed the Violence Against Women Act (VAWA). Since its passage, more than $130 million have been provided to the states to fund programs that assist victims of domestic violence and train law enforcement officers on how to respond to domestic violence calls. According to the National Coalition Against Domestic Violence (NCADV), VAWA has helped reduce the rate of domestic violence. Between 1993 and 1997, the rate of intimate partner violence fell from 9.8 to 7.5 per 1,000 women. The act was up for renewal in 2000.

For its advocates, VAWA is an essential tool in responding to domestic violence. NCADV argues that, while domestic violence rates have dropped since the law was passed, the problem still persists. Moreover, Patricia Ireland, the president of the National Organization for Women, asserts that VAWA is just one of the tools needed to ensure that women are safe. She observes: "The threat of violence colors the decisions women make every day. . . . The Violence Against Women Act of 1994 only begins to address the problem—we have much more work left to do."

Not everyone agrees with Ireland's opinion, however. Phyllis Schlafly, the president of the Eagle Forum, maintains that Congress did not have the right to pass the VAWA. She writes: "Congress has neither the constitutional authority nor the experience to ameliorate domestic relations problems." Patrick Fagan of the Heritage Foundation claims that the VAWA is an ineffective approach to ending domestic violence because it does not provide a strategy to rebuild families and end the culture of violence.

The Violence Against Women Act is one way society has responded to violence. In the following chapter, the authors consider other steps that can be taken to reduce the extent of violence in American society.

"*Gun control laws help stop crimes before they happen.*"

Stronger Gun Control Laws Will Reduce Violent Crime

Handgun Control

Handgun Control is an organization that campaigns for gun safety legislation. In the following viewpoint, the organization asserts that gun laws are successful in reducing violent crime. According to Handgun Control, laws such as the Brady Act, which requires background checks on gun buyers, have prevented four hundred thousand felons and other prohibited purchasers from buying handguns. The organization contends that the National Rifle Association (NRA) is wrong when it criticizes the enforcement of these laws and tries to prevent the passage of new gun laws.

As you read, consider the following questions:
1. On what issue do Handgun Control and the National Rifle Association agree?
2. According to Handgun Control, by what percentage has the number of inmates imprisoned on weapons or arson charges increased from 1993 to 1998?
3. How did the NRA stymie the investigation of the Littleton massacre, as stated by Handgun Control?

Reprinted from Handgun Control, "Preventing Crime and Prosecuting Criminals," available at www.handguncontrol.com/facts/ib/prevent.asp. Reprinted with permission from Handgun Control and the Center to Prevent Handgun Violence.

The NRA [National Rifle Association] likes to pass off the old cliché that "guns aren't the problem, it's the criminals who use guns who are the problem." Gun laws don't work, they argue. The real problem, they say, is not proliferation and easy accessibility of guns through loopholes in existing law, but that prosecution of gun crimes are down and existing laws are not being enforced. As usual, this is not the case. And as usual, the NRA only offers "get tough" punishments for criminals who have already committed gun crimes, without even considering how to keep guns away from criminals (or children) in the first place.

While Handgun Control and the NRA are frequently on the opposite sides of the debate on guns, we do agree on one issue: we should vigorously enforce the gun laws already on the books and punish criminals who use guns. The NRA supports Project Exile, a program pioneered in Richmond that increases federal prosecution of gun crime. Guess what? So does Handgun Control—and so do most gun control advocates, who see no contradiction between tough prevention and tough punishment. Unfortunately, the NRA offers punishment INSTEAD of prevention as their only argument. We believe that the fight against gun violence requires a comprehensive approach that includes getting tough on criminals who use guns, strictly enforcing existing gun laws AND enacting new laws to prevent first-time gun crimes and violence.

Preventing Gun Crimes Before They Happen

On March 24, 1998, firing from woods overlooking their school, 13-year-old Andrew Golden and 11-year-old Mitchell Johnson shot and killed four middle school students and a teacher and injured ten other students in Jonesboro, Arkansas. The two boys had a semiautomatic M-1 carbine with a large ammunition magazine, two other rifles, seven handguns and more than 500 rounds of ammunition which they took from the home of one of the boy's grandfather, who had a large arsenal of weapons left unsecured. Officers arrested the two boys as they ran through the wooded area near the school, and they were convicted on five counts of capital murder and ten counts of first-degree battery in September 1998.

Andrew Golden and Mitchell Johnson will be held at a juvenile detention facility until they turn 21 years old. Despite the fact that these two boys will be in prison for many years of their young lives, four children and a teacher are dead, their families' lives have been shattered forever and a community—and the rest of the nation—have been torn apart. But we must ask ourselves, could something have been done to keep these boys from getting the guns in the first place?

Gun control laws help stop crimes before they happen. For example, background checks, required by the Brady Act, have helped prevent potentially dangerous people from owning guns. According to the U.S. Department of Justice, since the Brady Law went into effect, background checks nationwide have stopped approximately 400,000 felons and other prohibited purchasers from buying handguns over-the-counter from federally licensed firearm dealers. What does this mean? Thousands of murders, spousal abusers, gun traffickers and fugitives from justice have been denied purchase of handguns and apprehended because of the background check required by the Brady Law.

In addition, control measures, like Child Access Prevention (CAP) laws, go a long way toward keeping guns out of the hands of children. CAP laws generally require adults to either store loaded guns in a place that is reasonably inaccessible to children, or use a device to lock the gun. If a child obtains an improperly stored, loaded gun, the adult owner is criminally liable.

Likewise, many of the tragedies that we read about every day can be prevented with stronger gun laws that make it tougher for kids and criminals to get guns. Although gun control legislation has succeeded in helping limit illegal firearm purchases, decrease gun-related crimes, deter criminal gun trafficking and reduce overall gun violence, gaping loopholes make our current laws inadequate for keeping guns away from children and criminals. Prosecutors and law enforcement nationwide have called for the closing of loopholes that allow guns to flow to children or criminals. Handgun Control supports new, common-sense legislation to build upon the success of the Brady Law and to strengthen our existing laws to keep guns from juveniles, convicted felons and other prohibited purchasers. To do this, we must close the loopholes that continue to allow the wrong people to get guns.

Firearm Prosecutions

The NRA complains that the laws on the books aren't being enforced. Wrong. Gun laws are enforced more vigorously today than five years ago, and overall firearms prosecutions are up. Prosecutions are more frequent than ever before; sentences are longer; and the number of inmates in prison on gun offenses is at a record level. The NRA's criticisms of federal prosecution statistics ignore the basic fact that both federal and state authorities prosecute gun cases, and federal authorities typically focus on the most serious type of offenders. Since more criminals who use guns are going to jail for longer sentences, it's clear that the gun lobby's attack on federal law enforcement efforts are meant to dodge a subject that they don't want to talk about—namely, gun control works to help reduce gun violence and stop children and criminals from getting guns in the first place.

• Since 1992, the total number of federal and state prose-

Scott Bateman. Reprinted with special permission of King Features Syndicate.

cutions has increased sharply—about 25 percent more criminals are sent to prison for state and federal weapon offenses than in 1992 (from 20,681 to 25,186).

• The number of higher-level offenders (those sentenced to five or more years) has gone up nearly 30 percent (from 1049 to 1345) in five years.

• The number of inmates in federal prison on firearm or arson charges (the two are counted together) increased 51 percent from 1993 to 1998, to a total of 8,979.

• In 1998, the Bureau of Alcohol Tobacco and Firearms brought 3,619 criminal cases involving 5,620 defendants to justice.

The Truth About the NRA

• The NRA has for years successfully blocked the computerization by the Bureau of Alcohol, Tobacco and Firearms (ATF) of gun sale records from out-of-business gun dealers. Thanks to the NRA-imposed restrictions, when a gun is traced as part of a criminal investigation, the files must often be retrieved manually from warehouses where the records are kept. As a result, hours or even days are added to the time needed to complete the successful trace of a crime gun. As a result, criminals avoid detection and criminal investigations are impeded.

• The NRA has maintained its steadfast opposition to waiting periods for handgun purchases, despite the need for a "cooling off" period to prevent impulse crimes and suicides. Because of NRA lobbyists, the waiting period included in the original Brady law expired in 1998, and the gun lobby is fighting efforts to reinstate it in 1999.

• The NRA likes to talk tough when it comes to criminals. But just this year, the NRA spent over $3.7 million to try to pass a referendum in Missouri, Proposition B, which would have allowed almost anyone, even convicted criminals with misdemeanor records, to carry a concealed weapon almost anywhere in the state. The referendum would have even permitted people convicted of stalking and child molestation the ability to carry a hidden handgun into bars, stadiums, parks, school yards and other public places. Fortunately, Missouri voters rejected Proposition B and the NRA's intense lobbying effort to put more guns on our streets.

• At every opportunity, the NRA has sought to decrease or eliminate the funding of the ATF, the law enforcement agency whose mission it is to oversee gun crimes and trace the guns used in the commission of crimes. Because of NRA-sponsored legislation, investigators seeking to trace the path of the guns used in the Littleton school massacre were forced to plod through paper records stretching among numerous states, culminating in a dead end at Colorado gun shows. Only through legwork and luck were investigators able to piece together how the four weapons ended up in the hands of the teenage shooters. The NRA continues to vociferously oppose any gun registration system that would allow law enforcement to retain records so as to easily trace guns used in crime.

• In 1986, the NRA got legislation passed which restricts ATF inspection of gun dealers to once a year. Even dealers who are the source for hundreds of crime guns cannot be routinely inspected more than once a year without a special court warrant. Of course, this is consistent with the NRA letter describing ATF as "jack-booted thugs," which caused former president George Bush to publicly resign his NRA membership in protest.

• As of April 1999, there were more than 100,000 federally licensed firearm dealers (FFL's) in America—more licensed gun dealers than there are McDonald's franchises. Yet there were only 1,783 ATF agents to police them; many of those agents are detailed by law to only investigate crimes involving explosives.

"The U.S., it would appear, is actually hindering not too many or too few handgun owners but the wrong ones."

Current Gun Control Laws Will Not Reduce Violent Crime

Edmund F. McGarrell

In the following viewpoint, Edmund F. McGarrell maintains that gun laws are ineffective at reducing violent crime because they focus too much on the number of guns that are in American society and not on who owns those guns. He claims that gun control laws, as currently written, are based on the faulty belief that societies with more guns experience more gun violence. McGarrell asserts that guns, if owned by law-abiding citizens, can in fact deter crime. He concludes that for gun control laws to be effective, they need to ease restrictions on legal possession and target illegal possession and use. McGarrell is the director of the Crime Control Policy Center at the Hudson Institute. The center looks for solutions to the problem of crime in Indianapolis.

As you read, consider the following questions:
1. According to the author, why do Sweden and Israel have low rates of gun crime, even though much of their citizenry is armed?
2. According to Gary Kleck, as cited by McGarrell, how much more common are defensive uses of a gun, compared to crimes involving a gun?
3. What are some of the programs the author cites as successfully targeting illegal firearms possession?

Excerpted from Edmund F. McGarrell, "More Guns, Less Crime," *American Outlook*, Fall 1999. Reprinted with permission from the author.

The events at Wedgwood Baptist Church in Fort Worth, Texas, and Columbine High School in Littleton, Colorado, coupled with other high-profile gun crimes in Los Angeles, suburban Chicago, Atlanta, and far too many other places, have instigated a new frenzy of debate over gun control legislation. Proponents of increased gun control, however, have always tended to argue from a particular set of assumptions rather than empirical evidence about what effective laws regulating guns and gun crime would actually look like. Consequently, any likely new additions to the more than twenty-thousand federal, state, and local laws governing firearms will almost certainly have little or no effect on gun-related crime. There is, however, a small but growing body of research that suggests a more effective approach to firearms crime is both possible and imminent.

The Connection Between Guns and Violence

Advocates for tighter restrictions on the purchase, possession, and carrying of guns by law-abiding citizens actually have scant evidence that new restrictions will reduce firearms deaths and injuries. Rather, their argument is based on the logic that because guns are often used to produce wrongful deaths and injuries, having fewer guns in circulation should reduce these incidents. The thesis makes intuitive sense, of course, and is consistent with what criminologists call the routine-activities explanation of crime. Routine-activities theorists study how lifestyle changes in communities or nations produce differences in the amount and nature of crime. Researchers have found, for example, that states enacting motorcycle-helmet laws experienced drops in motorcycle theft because of the increased risk that a would-be thief without a helmet would be stopped by the police and the theft discovered. Applying such reasoning to the issue of firearms violence, routine-activities theorists would predict that a society with more guns will experience more gun violence.

U.S. firearms-crime figures appear to support this perspective. The U.S. has a large number of firearms in circulation and high rates of violent crime. Yet, following an extensive review of the research on guns and crime, Florida State University criminologist Gary Kleck found, "Areas of the country that have high gun ownership rates do not, as a result, have higher violence rates." (See his book, *Targeting Guns: Firearms and Their Control,* Aldine de Gruyter, 1997.) Though this observation may initially seem puzzling, it is true of both gun crime and accidental shootings. Prevalence of firearms did relate to higher rates of suicide by firearm but not to overall suicide rates. It appears that a person bent on ending his life will simply use some other method if firearms are unavailable.

The picture becomes even more complex when comparing other nations. For those who argue that U.S. firearms-crime rates prove that the number of guns in a society determines the amount of gun crime, the experiences of countries like Switzerland and Israel are difficult to explain. In Switzerland, males between the ages of twenty and forty-two are *required* to have firearms at home, yet the country has a very low rate of violent gun crime. (All able-bodied Swiss males are part of the military reserve.) In Israel, likewise, all young citizens (that is, the very group most likely to commit crimes) are armed, yet there too the rate of violent crime is extremely low. In fact, World Health Organization data comparing fifty-two nations placed Switzerland and Israel as the twelfth and ninth safest countries in terms of homicides. Their rates are approximately one-seventh that of the U.S. One explanation for this disparity is that Switzerland and Israel generate extremely low rates of *illegal* firearm possession, whereas the U.S. focuses on the regulation of *legal* possession. The U.S., it would appear, is actually hindering not too many or too few handgun owners but *the wrong ones.*

The Effect of New Gun Laws

There are more than 230 million guns and an estimated fifty-nine million gun owners in the United States today. These guns and their owners generate less than one million gun crimes per year. Kleck estimates that 99.9 percent of gun-carrying does not result in a violent crime. These figures have several important implications. First, even if one finds the routine-activities perspective persuasive, the reality is that new laws are unlikely to alter the large stock of firearms now in circulation. Second, new laws are more likely to affect legal gun owners than illegal owners and users. The bumper sticker "If guns are outlawed, only outlaws will have guns," though much derided by gun-control advocates, certainly suggests the limits of new restrictions: Does anyone seriously doubt that law-abiding citizens are more likely than criminals to comply with gun laws? Third, new gun law's must either be aimed at the overwhelming number of guns and owners that will never be involved in a crime, with the hope that they will also target the tiny fraction of illegal users, or they must be finely tuned to distinguish between legal and illegal possession and use. Thus the most important question to ask of any gun-control proposal being considered in today's debate is the very one not being asked now: how the proposed law distinguishes between legal and illegal gun ownership.

Legal Possession and Defensive Use

John Lott, a fellow in economics and law at the University of Chicago, and Gary Kleck have drawn the ire of many criminologists and gun-control advocates by reporting research findings suggesting that the possession of firearms by law-abiding citizens may actually reduce crime. Kleck has challenged the effectiveness of many gun-control measures and provided evidence that guns are used far more often for defensive purposes than they are for carrying out a crime. In fact, he estimates that defensive uses of a gun by potential victims to prevent crimes are approximately three times as common as crimes involving a gun.

Lott has generated considerable controversy by suggesting that increased levels of legal gun carrying may reduce crime by acting as a deterrent to prospective offenders. (See his controversial book, *More Guns, Less Crime: Understanding Crime and Gun Control Laws*, University of Chicago Press, 1998.) Lott and colleague David Mustard analyzed crime trends in more than three-thousand counties across the U.S., comparing counties where "shall issue" laws were enacted with counties operating with more restrictive provisions governing gun permits. (See John R. Lott and David Mustard, "Crime, Deterrence, and Right-to-Carry Concealed Handguns," *Journal of Legal Studies* 26 (1997): 1-68;

and John R. Lott, "Gun Laws Can Be Dangerous, Too," *The Wall Street Journal*, May 12, 1999.) Shall-issue provisions instruct law enforcement agencies to issue a permit for carrying a concealed weapon unless the individual is ineligible based on specific legal criteria. The intent of such laws is to allow law-abiding adults to carry concealed weapons.

How Guns Can Reduce Crime

While support for strict gun-control laws usually has been strongest in large cities, where crime rates are highest, that's precisely where right-to-carry laws have produced the largest drops in violent crimes. For example, in counties with populations of more than 200,000 people, concealed-handgun laws produced an average drop in murder rates of more than 13%. The half of the counties with the highest rape rates saw that crime drop by more than 7%.

John R. Lott Jr., *LEAA Advocate*, Winter 1997.

Reflecting the routine-activities theory, critics of shall-issue laws predicted that the larger number of citizens carrying firearms would lead to a greater amount of firearms violence. The increased number of weapons, they contended, would cause everyday disputes to erupt into gun violence. Lott's research, however, has shown just the opposite. Violent crime decreased in counties where shall-issue laws were enacted, and the results were statistically significant when contrasted with the trend in counties without these laws. Lott plausibly infers that potential offenders are deterred by the increased possibility that an intended victim of crime may be carrying a firearm.

There was also no increase in accidental deaths in the shall-issue counties. Currently, approximately thirty to forty youths aged five and under die from the accidental discharge of a firearm each year. Although even one is too many, this compares to approximately 150 who die from fires they start with cigarette lighters and is less than the number who drown in water buckets. (See Morgan Reynolds and H. Sterling Burnett, "Gun Control Frenzy," *Washington Times*, June 15, 1999, and John Lott's *Wall Street Journal* article mentioned earlier.) Thus current research suggests that increasing the number of legally carried guns in circulation can reduce crime without any bad side effects.

Targeting Illegal Possession

In contrast to the lack of evidence for the effectiveness of general restrictions on crime reduction, there is a growing body of research suggesting that aggressive enforcement targeted at illegal possession and use of firearms can significantly reduce violent gun crime. Examples of such success include the New York City Police Department's aggressive enforcement of illegal-gun-carrying statutes; Boston's targeted enforcement of violent youth gangs; and Richmond's Project Exile involving federal prosecution of all felons caught with firearms. All three cities have experienced significant declines in violent gun crime. Additional evidence from the Hudson Institute shows that directed police patrols aimed at high-risk individuals at high-crime locations produce significant drops in gun crime. Current Hudson research in Indianapolis also indicates that the Boston-style effort of targeting groups of known chronic offenders is reducing homicides there. (For more details on these studies, see my article "Crime Must Have a Stop," in the Summer 1999 *American Outlook*.)

Combining the Kleck and Lott findings with the research on targeting illegal users of firearms reveals an interesting relationship between legal and illegal firearms possession. Specifically, firearms crime may best be addressed by the following means: easing restrictions on *legal* possession, targeting *illegal* possession and use, and simultaneously increasing legal possession while decreasing illegal possession.

"*Zero tolerance policies are far from perfect, but they're working in thousands of school districts today.*"

Zero Tolerance Policies Are a Useful Response to School Violence

Vincent L. Ferrandino and Gerald N. Tirozzi

In the following viewpoint, Vincent L. Ferrandino and Gerald N. Tirozzi contend that while zero tolerance is not perfect, it remains the best solution to reducing school violence. The authors acknowledge that such policies should be refined in order to take into consideration the age of the perpetrator and the seriousness of the crime. However, they argue, the media tend to overemphasize the problems caused by zero-tolerance policies and ignore their benefits. Ferrandino is the executive director of the National Association of Elementary School Principals. Tirozzi is the executive director of the National Association of Secondary School Principals.

As you read, consider the following questions:
1. When did zero tolerance emerge, as stated by the authors?
2. According to Ferrandino and Tirozzi, why is defending zero tolerance policies a conundrum for school principals?
3. What do the authors see as "students' rights"?

Excerpted from Vincent L. Ferrandino and Gerald N. Tirozzi, "Zero Tolerance: A Win-Lose Policy," *Education Week*, January 26, 2000. Reprinted with permission from the authors.

Every school day, principals struggle to protect youngsters while at the same time working to make sure they receive the best education possible. We cannot tolerate violence against our students and staffs. We must be thoughtful but aggressive, with clear policies that are understood by students and their parents. These policies must be fairly administered with due process assurances in place.

However, we may want to refine our policies to make sure they address three critical areas:

• consideration should be given for age and grade level;
• the punishment should fit the "crime"; and
• educational services should never stop.

Both the National Association of Elementary School Principals (NAESP) and the National Association of Secondary School Principals (NASSP) support bills in the House and Senate that would require states and schools to provide alternative educational services, supervision, and counseling for any student who is expelled.

We must also be honest and fair. If a mistake is made or a reaction is too severe, we should admit it and work to correct it. However, we should not have to apologize for upholding our communities' expectations for safe, orderly, and drug-free schools.

The Origins of Zero Tolerance Policies

Zero tolerance is not new, and it didn't start in schools. In fact, it emerged in the 1980s as states and the federal government fought illegal drugs. Soon after, school systems began using similar policies in their fight against drugs.

By 1994, the Safe- and Drug-Free Schools and Communities Act required schools that received federal funds to expel students who brought weapons or drugs to school. During this time public opinion polls began saying that schools were seen as unsafe and undisciplined. Americans were demanding that schools do whatever it took to assure students' safety.

In response, school districts spent a great deal of time, effort, and funds on everything from conflict resolution programs to metal detectors. They also broadened their zero tolerance policies to include harassment, fighting, gang activity, toy weapons, any drugs, threats of violence, and hate offenses.

Media Attacks

Defending zero tolerance policies represents a conundrum for school principals. On the one hand, principals are expected to protect all students in schools and clearly articulate the type of behavior that is not acceptable. At the same time, the press seems to be unrelenting and vociferous in its attacks on school principals for enforcing these policies. Zero tolerance was again thrown into the national spotlight when six high school students from Decatur, Illinois, were expelled for brawling. Immediately, the print, broadcast, and Internet editorialists rehashed every news-making zero tolerance incident—children suspended or expelled for bringing nail clippers or mouthwash to school, for scribbling threats or scary messages, for writing horror stories, and so on—in which principals had followed their school board policies and/or procedures.

Making Zero Tolerance Work

In order for zero tolerance to work, there are four basic conditions that must be present:

1. Clear consequences for misbehavior, with consistency of application;

2. Collaborative development by all stake-holding agencies of an alternative education system;

3. Knowledge of zero tolerance experience in other states, districts or schools; and

4. Integration of sequential and comprehensive health education programs that include drug and alcohol curricula.

Frank E. Blair, *Principal Magazine*, September 1999.

Ironically, almost no news reports praised schools for their safety efforts. Little was heard of how many dangerous incidents at schools had been avoided, or whether students felt safer as a result of these get-tough policies. Instead, schools were accused of taking the easy way out, hiding behind their rules, and using a one-size-fits-all approach to discipline. Papers were full of phrases like "draconian punishment" and "zero tolerance, zero sense." Accusations that school authorities "ignored the needs of these troubled youth" or that schools were "scared stupid" surfaced on TV and in syndicated columns.

The Best Solution

Do the outraged media have a point? Of course. Should we take another look at zero tolerance and put back some professional judgment in the decision making? Yes.

Is there a better way to assure safety for all students and prevent random acts of violence? Not yet! All the studies by law enforcement agencies (including the FBI and Secret Service), think tank reports, safety summits, government decrees, and a minor industry that has developed around school safety, have yet to find that way.

If ever there was a time to support the outstanding women and men who are providing tireless and conscientious leadership to insure safe, orderly, and drug-free environments, now is that time! The press and others make a case for students' rights. We too believe strongly in students' rights as clearly stated in our Declaration of Independence—life, liberty, and the pursuit of happiness. Above all else, students have a right to live!

Zero tolerance policies are far from perfect, but they're working in thousands of school districts today. We believe they send a strong message that helps students feel safe in school. The very moment that this society becomes safe for our children, we'll be delighted to zero out zero tolerance in our nation's schools.

"Zero tolerance, despite its appearance of fairness, is inherently an unfair policy."

Zero Tolerance Policies Are an Unfair Response to School Violence

Richard L. Curwin and Allen N. Mendler

In the following viewpoint, Richard L. Curwin and Allen N. Mendler argue that zero tolerance policies are the wrong approach to reducing school violence because such policies require suspensions or expulsions even when not appropriate. They cite examples in which schools have ignored the extenuating circumstances when a student broke a zero tolerance policy, for example by bringing a gun to school. Curwin and Mendler contend that a better response to school violence is a "tough as necessary" policy, in which the consequences for misbehavior can range from mild to severe and where circumstances are taken into account. Curwin and Mendler are the coauthors of *Discipline with Dignity* and the founders of Discipline Associates, where they teach educators and administrators how to manage behavior and improve student responsibility.

As you read, consider the following questions:

1. In the authors' view, why is eliminating zero tolerance policies a tough sell?
2. How do the authors define strength?
3. What are some of the consequences Curwin and Mendler list for their "tough but necessary" policy?

Reprinted from Richard L. Curwin and Allen N. Mendler, "Zero Tolerance for Zero Tolerance," *Kappan Professional Journal*, October 1999. Reprinted with permission from Richard L. Curwin. More information may be found at www.disciplineassociates.com.

Zero tolerance is another example of the road to hell paved with good intentions. What was originally intended as a policy to improve safety in school by ensuring that all children—regardless of race, athletic ability, or parental influence—follow the rules is used now as an excuse to treat all children the same when they are in need of corrective measures. Schools should have zero tolerance for the idea of doing anything that treats all students the same. One size does not and cannot fit all. The well-investigated research of Russ Skiba and Reece Peterson clearly demonstrates just how ineffective and full of false assumptions the concept of zero tolerance is.

We agree that zero tolerance sends a powerful message to the school community that violent, aggressive behavior will not be tolerated. We need strong, effective policies to protect our students and to help them feel safe. However, zero tolerance, despite its appearance of fairness, is inherently an unfair policy. A doctor is not fair if he prescribes chemotherapy for two patients with headaches—one with a brain tumor and the other with a sinus condition—regardless of the similarity of symptoms. When two students in school throw a pencil—one because he has finished his assignment and is bored, the other because he cannot read the directions and thus hasn't even started the assignment—we do not treat them the same, regardless of the behavioral similarity. Any intervention that treats dissimilar problems with similar behavioral outcomes the same is not only unfair but destined to fail.

Eliminating zero tolerance policies is a hard sell because the concept is simple to understand, sounds tough, and gives the impression of high standards for behavior. Yet these very characteristics actually make things worse in many cases. Any intervention for changing children's behavior that is simple is simple-minded, and those that substitute formulas for decisions made by people who understand the circumstances are dangerous. It's time for schools to develop legitimate high standards by refusing to fall for the lure of what is easy and sounds good and choosing instead what is truly best for children.

We call our solution "as tough as necessary," an approach that finds the balance between being strong and being fair.

In some cases, the toughness required might be stronger than a previous zero tolerance solution. In other cases, the solution might involve other alternatives, including counseling, parent involvement, conflict resolution, training, or planning. The new synthesis sends this message: violence will not be tolerated, and yet we will not deal with students as if they are fast food. We can meet their needs without resorting to formulas while still protecting the school and its inhabitants from unacceptable behavior.

Zero Tolerance Policies Can Create More Problems

Most educators, community members, and parents would agree that leaving disengaged, disruptive, or troubled youth to their own devices for a large part of the day is not a good idea, but this result is essentially the impact of zero tolerance policies throughout the country. Deborah Prothrow-Stith of Harvard University notes, "I don't have a lot of patience for professionals who buy into this get-tough, kick-them-out mentality, because they know it doesn't work." She goes on to say that a policy that puts student offenders into the community may cause more havoc by relocating the problem to the criminal justice system, making suspensions more expensive in the long run.

Anne S. Robertson, *Parent News*, March/April 2000.

It is readily apparent that as tough as necessary is far superior to zero tolerance if we examine each policy in terms of how it teaches children to behave. Would anyone want a school board or a superintendent who had a zero tolerance attitude when dealing with stakeholders? Do you know anyone who was raised by a zero tolerant parent? What might that person say about how it affected his or her childhood? Could a marriage survive a zero tolerant spouse? More important, do we want children to have zero tolerance for others, particularly when they are angry?

How Zero Tolerance Can Be Problematic

We do not question the need for clear, firm limits or the conviction that certain behaviors are not acceptable. As tough as necessary allows us to honor and enforce limits without modeling "no tolerance." We would much rather see children who are as tough as necessary than ones who are zero tolerant. The following two case studies support our position. In the first, a young high school student was expelled after bringing a gun to school. Should he have been? That morning, his father, in a drunken rage, had put a gun down the youngster's throat and, before passing out, threatened to kill him and his younger brother. The student brought the gun to school to save their lives. Before he could give it to his principal, the gun was discovered. No amount of explaining helped because of zero tolerance. We are not advocating guns in school, but we want ways of preventing them legitimately without fostering foolish behavior.

In the second case, a young man was suspended from school for violating the three-cut policy by missing his family living class. On investigating the situation, a caring teacher discovered the reason behind the boy's behavior. Whenever his mother, a crack cocaine addict, received her government check, she cashed it and bought cocaine within minutes. This fine young man started waiting outside for the mailman in all types of weather. He intercepted the check, took it to the issuing bank, and waited for the manager, who gave him cash in envelopes. He took one envelope to pay the rent, another for food, another for utilities, and so on, until all the family's bills were paid. By the time he arrived at school, he had missed family living. Should he be suspended or given a medal for holding his family together?

Some might argue that no excuses can ever be accepted because they weaken the system and provide loopholes for the less honorable. We see no strength in a system that uses the already frail, those least able to benefit, as sacrificial lambs. We define strength as strength of character, of values, and of clarity.

Tough as Necessary

To establish an as tough as necessary policy, schools and individual teachers begin by discussing values, especially those related to safety. All members of the school community—teachers, administrators, students, paraprofessionals, and parents—need to contribute to the general guidelines.

1. School will be safe.
2. We resolve our differences through talking, not fighting.
3. We are all responsible for preventing violent behavior.
4. We care for and protect one another's person, property, and feelings.

From these guidelines, the school community develops its rules.

1. No weapons allowed in school.
2. We do not touch one another without permission.
3. We report when we hear of a fight brewing.

The final step is to establish consequences that take into account a wide range of circumstances. The consequences must cover a spectrum from the mildest to the most severe, including filing police charges. Only then will the school have the options necessary to meet the needs of the rule violator, other students, and all those who work in the school. Examples of consequences include counseling, restitution, behavioral planning, behavior rehearsal, suspension with training or educational experience, and police referral.

Zero tolerance was developed in response to legitimate concerns that cannot be ignored. However, when the solution creates more difficulty than the original problem, it is time to abandon it for something better. As tough as necessary is the best answer.

"The principle targets of hate-crimes legislation are organized forms of hostility and the violence that these directly promote."

Hate-Crimes Laws Are a Solution to Violence Against Minorities

Jeffrey C. Isaac

Hate-crimes laws are a necessary response to violence against minorities, Jeffrey C. Isaac claims in the following viewpoint. He cites a shooting spree by Benjamin Smith, a man who belonged to a neo-Nazi organization, as an example of the violence that needs to be targeted. According to Isaac, hate crimes are a serious problem that should not be considered an occasional aberration. Isaac is a professor of political science at Indiana University in Bloomington and the director of the Center for the Study of Democracy and Public Life at the university.

As you read, consider the following questions:

1. According to the author, what incident led to the formation of Bloomington United?
2. What does Andrew Sullivan conclude about hate crimes, as stated by Isaac?
3. In Isaac's opinion, what is the advantage of well-written hate-crimes laws?

Reprinted from Jeffrey C. Isaac, "Responding to Hate," *Dissent*, Winter 2000. Reprinted with permission from *Dissent*.

I had always been sympathetic toward the Anti-Defamation League (ADL) and the Southern Poverty Law Center. As a Jew whose father's family had been murdered during the Holocaust, and as someone on "the left" for whom the civil rights movement was a decisive moment of contemporary politics, I could not help but support organizations that monitored and opposed so-called "hate groups" like the KKK and the Aryan Nation. But these issues never engaged me deeply. The hate groups seemed utterly marginal in American life. And the question of whether or not to be against them never struck me as interesting. If asked, I would answer "of course I oppose them," and then I would proceed to read about and talk about all the "bigger" questions—about capitalism, liberalism, democracy, civil society.

A Hate Crime in Indiana

Then, in July of 1998, I woke up one morning to discover that sections of the college town in which I live—Bloomington, Indiana—had been blanketed with vicious anti-Semitic and racist literature. I was shocked, as were many of my friends and neighbors. After a number of such incidents some of us felt the need to respond in a serious way to this leafleting, which was politically revolting but also threatening to many, especially Jews and people of color, who were singled out in inflammatory ways by the leaflets. Before long an ad hoc community group called Bloomington United was formed. We ran ads in the local newspaper condemning the expressions of hate. We raised a few thousand dollars to produce cardboard signs that read "Bloomington United. No Hate Speech. No Hate Crimes. Not in our Yards. Not in our Town. Not Anywhere." The community outpouring of support was tremendous. Thousands of signs went up all over town. We organized a march, joined by more than a thousand people, from the campus of Indiana University to the town square, where for over an hour speakers including the mayor, an African-American minister representing the United Methodist Church, the rabbi of the only synagogue in town, and representatives of the gay community and the labor movement spoke out in favor of civility and equal respect.

Bloomington United brought together leaders from the

Jewish community, the gay/lesbian/transgendered community, the African-American community, and a wide range of citizens. It helped to organize study circles on race. It sought connections with the public schools. And then, on the weekend of July 4, 1999, the young man who had been distributing the neo-nazi literature—one Benjamin "August" Smith, a "representative" of the neo-nazi World Church of the Creator—went on a shooting spree that left two people dead and eleven others injured. One of those killed was a Korean graduate student at Indiana University, WonJoon Yoon, who was shot while standing outside Bloomington's only Korean church. The community responded with a "Gathering of Healing." More than three thousand people attended, a standing-room-only crowd, with people of all ages, races, and religions spilling outside the hall. The mayor spoke. IU's vice-chancellor spoke, followed by the Hillel rabbi, and by Janet Reno. It was a moving event, and in its wake Bloomington United continues to function as a symbol of democratic civility and as a respected community group. Indeed, one of my leftist friends in the university has gone so far as to describe Bloomington United as "the largest social movement" in the recent history of Bloomington.

Like any social movement, Bloomington United is a diverse group. It has grappled with some thorny issues related to the representation of specific groups—Asians and Asian Americans, African Americans, Jewish Americans, and especially gays—and it has thus far navigated these successfully. It has confronted criticisms from segments of the African-American campus community for worrying too much about hate groups and not enough about broader issues of racism. It has confronted criticisms for being too "liberal," for preaching to the converted, and for failing to organize lower-class whites in the hinterlands of Southern Indiana. And it has sought to address these challenges and criticisms, making adjustments when necessary.

Responding to Criticisms

In the course of this activity I learned that the issues of hate, hate groups, and hate crimes are very real, that they are capable of shocking and galvanizing a community, and that they are inextricably related to the "bigger" issues that we on the left typically and rightfully address—issues like racism, class inequality and resentment, media violence, and the accessibility of dangerous weapons. But efforts like Bloomington United draw their energy from their specificity, and it is sometimes important to make the connections but not make them too sharply. Bloomington United includes labor people and the president of the Bloomington Chamber of Commerce, who is one of the most important activists. It includes leaders of the gay community and religious people whose churches are uncomfortable with homosexuality. That is its strength. There is a politics here, and it is a politics of inclusivity and democratic civility that has the potential to radiate out onto other issues. But it is also a very specific kind of politics, an ad hoc civic initiative that avoids strong ideological definition.

As a participant, I have found it both publicly necessary and intellectually challenging to explain this politics and to respond to some of the unfair criticisms of it, often made by individuals who have stood on the sidelines. Many of these criticisms were echoed this fall in a piece published in the *New York Times Sunday Magazine* by Andrew Sullivan, "What's So Bad About Hate?" Sullivan argues that the motivations behind hate are various and that the subjective experience of hate takes different forms and has different effects depending on who is acting it out. His conclusion: the preoccupation with hate is overstated and sentimental, there is really no intellectually respectable way to distinguish hate crimes from other crimes; and hate-crimes laws can only have pernicious effects.

Sullivan's argument is powerful, but only because he insists on interpreting "hate" the way much of the sentimental discourse he criticizes interprets it—in subjective, purely experiential terms, as a personal feeling or passion. If only we can make people feel nicer toward one another, we could eliminate hate; Sullivan is rightly suspicious of the legislation of niceness. But behind this admittedly sentimental way of thinking about hate lies a very real, historical and political phenomenon—the activities of hate groups, mainly, though not exclusively, right-wing organizations that systematically promote hostility toward racial, religious, and sexual minorities that talk about and plan "racial holy wars"; and that offer various forms of military and paramilitary inspiration and training to their members, supporters, and fellow travelers.

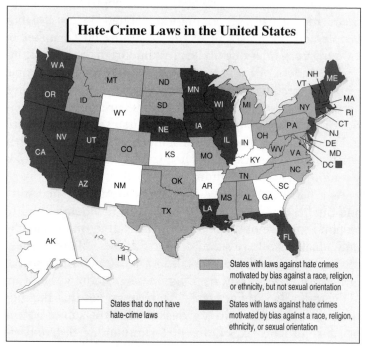

Hate-Crime Laws in the United States

States with laws against hate crimes motivated by bias against a race, religion, or ethnicity, but not sexual orientation

States that do not have hate-crime laws

States with laws against hate crimes motivated by bias against a race, religion, ethnicity, or sexual orientation

Facts On File News Services, 1998.

Sullivan conveniently downplays this phenomenon. He describes it as "mercifully rare" in the United States, writing it off as the province of sociopaths and psychopaths with no "widespread" influence. These hate groups do comprise only a small number of people, and I agree that they constitute "a deranged fringe of an American subculture." Still, the groups are real, and the subculture that generates them is equally real, and it ought not to be dismissed or written off as some psychopathological aberration. This is borne out by the ADL's report *Poisoning the Web*, and by the literature of the Southern Poverty Law Center and the Center for New Community, to name but a few of the many national organizations and community groups that monitor the activities of hate groups. And it is borne out by what happened in Bloomington, and not only in Bloomington. Hate groups are a disturbingly palpable, objective phenomenon. The advantage of well-written hate-crimes laws is that under certain circumstances they make these organizations the legitimate subjects of criminal law enforcement and that the elevated penalties they prescribe make it very costly for individuals to act on their hatred by doing violence to the property and/or persons of targeted minority groups.

The Targets of Hate-Crimes Laws

There are legitimate civil liberties concerns about such laws, though serious organizations, most notably the ADL, have sought to address them in their model legislation. But it is simply not true that the targets of such legislation—hate crimes—are nebulous, subjective experiences. The principal targets of hate-crimes legislation are organized forms of hostility and the violence that these directly promote. There is a politics behind this legal discourse about hate crimes. It is a politics fraught with the dangers of one-upmanship and competitive vulnerability. But it is a serious politics not reducible to these, and it uses the law as one strategy among others to address a very real and frightening social and political phenomenon: the organizations that use money, media, and weapons to aid and abet the murderous actions of people like Benjamin Smith.

I am sometimes asked why we in Bloomington United have been making such an issue of hate. My answer is simple. We have not chosen to make an issue of hate. Hate has chosen to come to Bloomington and it has made an issue of us. Responding to hate is by no means the only thing worth doing, but it is important to do it.

> "Hate crime provisions seem vaguely
> directed at capturing a sense of cold-
> bloodedness, but the law can do that
> without elevating some victims over
> others."

Hate-Crimes Laws Are Too Arbitrary

Ann Coulter

Hate-crimes laws are the wrong approach to reducing violence because they are applied to inconsistently, Ann Coulter
contends in the following viewpoint. She cites cases in which
the murders committed by African American assailants against
white victims were ruled hate crimes, whereas the racist beliefs
of whites who killed African Americans were not considered.
She argues that the effect of these laws is to elevate some victims above others, even if the crimes are equally violent. Coulter also notes that hate-crimes laws are troubling because they
probe a defendant's thoughts and beliefs. Coulter is a syndicated columnist.

As you read, consider the following questions:
1. According to Coulter, what was the Supreme Court's
   reasoning for ignoring the defendant's membership in
   the Aryan Brotherhood in the case *Dawson v. Delaware*?
2. What is the "paradox of discrimination law," in the
   author's opinion?
3. According to the author, what do "state of mind"
   elements of a crime try to measure?

Reprinted from Ann Coulter, "Love Crimes," *Human Events*, December 17, 1999.
Reprinted with permission from *Human Events*.

The Supreme Court has had occasion to consider the constitutionality of "hate" as a factor in state criminal laws in four major cases. See if you detect a pattern.

Four Key Cases

• In *Barclay v. Florida*, 463 U.S. 939 (1983) (plurality opinion), a black man was convicted of murdering a white man. The question before the court was whether the murderer's membership in the Black Liberation Army (BLA) and desire to provoke a "race war" could be taken into account by the sentencing judge in determining whether to impose the death penalty.

The Supreme Court held that the defendant's membership in the BLA could be considered during sentencing because "the elements of racial hatred in [the] murder" pertained to several permissible aggravating factors.

• In *Dawson v. Delaware*, 503 U.S. 159 (1992) the state sought to introduce evidence of the defendant's membership in the Aryan Brotherhood at a capital sentencing hearing. This the Supreme Court ruled out of order, on the grounds that admission of the evidence violated the defendant's 1st Amendment rights because it "proved nothing more than [the defendant's] abstract beliefs."

• In *R.A.V. v. City of St. Paul*, 505 U.S, 377 (1992) the (presumably nonblack) defendant was accused of burning a cross on a black family's lawn and charged under the St. Paul, Minn., "Bias-Motivated Crime Ordinance," which made it a misdemeanor to place on public or private property "a symbol, object, appellation, characterization or graffiti, including, but not limited to, a burning cross or Nazi swastika, which one knows or has reasonable grounds to know arouses anger, alarm or resentment in others on the basis of race, color, creed, religion or gender."

In this case, the Supreme Court struck down the law as a content-based restriction on free speech.

• In *Wisconsin v. Mitchell*, 508 U.S. 476 (1993) the court considered the 1st Amendment rights of a black man charged in the brutal beating of a young boy, a beating that left the boy in a coma for several days. Just before the attack, the defendant and his friends were discussing a scene from the movie *Mississippi Burning* in which a white man beats a young black boy who is praying. The defendant concluded the discussion by saying: "Do you all feel hyped up to move on some white people?" Soon thereafter, when he saw a young white boy on the other side of the street, the defendant said: "You all want to f— somebody up? There goes a white boy; go get him."

In *Mitchell*, the Supreme Court held that evidence of the defendant's racial animus toward whites could be used to enhance his sentence from two years to four years.

When Government Ranks Crimes

Now before you rush out and beat someone senseless, there are differences among these cases, the holdings, the lawyers who argued them, and the personnel on the courts that decided them. But still, it is a striking fact that in the two cases in which the criminals were white racists and the victims black, evidence of the defendants beliefs was excluded; and in the two cases in which the defendants were blacks, evidence of their beliefs was deemed relevant.

That's one of the problems with "hate crimes," "bias crimes," or any crimes that are defined by the beliefs of the defendant. When the government ranks crimes by the political unpopularity of the perpetrator, it will inevitably lead to suspicions that, some defendants (and some victims) are more equal than others. Obviously this is not to suggest that the justices secretly sympathized with the White supremacists in these cases. It is to say the government should be out of the business of allowing speech to be a crime.

That's why the 1st Amendment "[a]bove all else," as Justice Thurgood Marshall declared, "means that government has no power to restrict expression because of its message, its ideas, its subject matter or its content." (*Chicago Police Department v. Mosely*)

It's easy to see that the government cannot prohibit a person from holding stupid or hateful beliefs. It's easy to see that the government cannot prohibit a person from passing out pamphlets or otherwise publicizing those views. But for some reason, it's much harder for people to comprehend that punishing a person for his beliefs while simultaneously punishing him for, say, murder, is also something the government cannot do. An unconstitutional law is no less unlawful when in the company of a constitutional law.

Elevating Certain Victims

Grisly murders by remorseless killers such as the murders of Matthew Shepard and James Byrd, Jr., do seem to deserve enhanced penalties. That's why the law permits increased punishment for crimes that are grisly and for criminals who are remorseless.

Shepard was beaten, tied to a fence, and left to die. Byrd was chained to the back of a pickup truck and dragged to his death, being decapitated along the way. What sort of motive could put these acts in a better light? If Shepard had been straight and Byrd white, would that make the crimes more palatable?

Hate crime provisions seem vaguely directed at capturing a sense of cold-bloodedness, but the law can do that without elevating some victims over others.

The paradox of discrimination law is that once a victim group has enough leverage to win special protection under the law, the law hardly seems necessary.

The federal sentencing guidelines increase penalties for crimes in which the defendant "intentionally selected any victim or any property as the object of the offense of conviction because of the actual or perceived race, color, religion, national origin, ethnicity, gender, disability, or sexual orientation of any person."

What if the defendant intentionally selected his victims because of what they were wearing? Or because they were Republicans? Aren't those victim selection methods equally cold-blooded?

Hate Crime Laws Result in Inequality

If the idea of hate crime statutes is to capture a level of ruthlessness, it doesn't make much sense to limit the list of protected characteristics—particularly when the characteristics chosen are distinguishable only in that they refer to organized groups with political muscle.

The inevitable result is that some victims are more equal

under the law than others. If gay rights advocates and anti-gay protestors rallied at the same site, and fights broke out between the two sides, only the anti-gay rights protestors could be tried for committing "hate crimes."

One Harvard law professor has argued that the criminal law already discriminates against some viewpoints by permitting proof of certain states of mind—such as "heat of passion"—to reduce a murder sentence to manslaughter. Because provocation is determined according to "modern understandings of provocation and passion, " Harvard Prof. Carol Steiker argues that these elements reinforce widely held viewpoints.

Hate Crimes and Homosexuality

The admitted purpose of gay agitation for hate-crime laws is to have homosexual acts (which in the real world define "sexual orientation") put on a par with religion, race, gender, and age as a legally protected category. There are many good reasons for thinking that a bad idea. But the very idea of "hate crimes" is highly dubious. Hate is a sin for which people may go to Hell. It is quite another thing to make it a crime for which people should go to jail.

Richard John Neuhaus, *First Things*, January 1999.

Prof. Steiker observes, for example, that a jury would likely reduce the murder charge of a man was provoked by finding his wife in bed with another man, but not that of a white supremacist who "becomes enraged and kills when he discovers that his daughter is romantically involved with a black man."

These are the kinds of dazzling distinctions they teach you to draw at Harvard Law School.

Consequently, Prof. Steiker concludes, the "law's choice to mitigate the latter killing itself inscribes . . . deeply held views about the proper roles of men and women in intimate relationships."

On that theory, the "reasonable man" standard would have to be excised root and branch from the law on the grounds that feminists are incapable of being reasonable.

Admittedly, aggravating and mitigating factors such as premeditation, provocation and self-defense assume that the defendant is a human being. And maybe that does constitute viewpoint discrimination against space aliens, farm animals and Hillary Clinton. But beyond that, the "state of mind" elements of a crime simply attempt to measure the malevolence of the crime, not the criminal's larger sociological views.

The Creepiest Aspects

A man who killed upon finding his wife in bed with another man, or because be was being attacked in a bar fight would not be questioned about his general position on adultery or his views on alcohol. By contrast, hate crime laws do not limit themselves to the defendant's state of mind at the moment of committing the crime, but insist on probing defendant's overall belief system.

This is the creepiest aspect of hate crime prosecutions: They have the ring of the thought police. A defendant's books, organizations, friends, all become relevant evidence. In a "hate crime" prosecution in Ohio, for example, *State v. Wyant*, the young white male defendant took the stand in order to testify that he frequently associated with black people. He was rigorously cross-examined by the prosecutor who asked the defendant questions such as whether he had ever gone to the movies or had a beer with his black neighbor, a 65-year-old black woman.

In *State v. Avers*, a Maryland "hate crime" case, the defendant was accused of viciously attacking two black women. He admitted to the attack, but repeatedly insisted he was not a racist, even producing four black friends who earnestly testified to that effect. Nonetheless, he was sentenced to an extra 20 years in prison for having chosen his victims allegedly because of their race.

One wonders why the defendant was not accused of choosing his victims on the basis of their gender. Perhaps women do not have enough pull in Maryland to force the legislature to criminalize hatred against them. It takes a lot of clout to be a victim.

Periodical Bibliography

The following articles have been selected to supplement the diverse views presented in this chapter. Addresses are provided for periodicals not indexed in the *Readers' Guide to Periodical Literature*, the *Alternative Press Index*, the *Social Sciences Index*, or the *Index to Legal Periodicals and Books*.

International Socialist Review	"The Politics of Hate Crimes," Fall 1999.
Issues and Controversies On File	"Hate-Crime Laws," December 25, 1998. Available from Facts On File News Services, 11 Penn Plaza, New York, NY, 10001.
Derrick Z. Jackson	"A Worthier Battle for Parents of School Shooting Victims," *Liberal Opinion Week*, November 15, 1999. Available from PO Box 880, Vinton, IA 52349-0880.
Kathy Koch	"Zero Tolerance," *CQ Researcher*, March 10, 2000. Available from 1414 22nd St. NW, Washington, DC 20037.
Lynne Lamberg	"Preventing School Violence: No Easy Answers," *JAMA*, August 5, 1998. Available from 515 N. State St., Chicago, IL 60610.
Eli Lehrer	"From Punching Bags into Body Bags?" *Insight on the News*, February 15, 1999. Available from 3600 New York Ave. NE, Washington, DC 20002.
John R. Lott Jr.	"How to Stop Mass Shootings," *American Enterprise*, July/August 1998.
Salim Muwakkil	"Juvenile Crime, Adult Time," *In These Times*, February 7, 2000.
Susan Raffo	"Thinking About Hate Crimes," *Z Magazine*, January 1999.
Judith Resnik	"Citizenship and Violence," *American Prospect*, March 27–April 10, 2000.
Kevin Sack	"Schools Add Security and Tighten Dress, Speech and Civility Rules," *The New York Times*, May 24, 1999.
Jeffrey Snyder	"Consumers of Safety," *Liberty*, July 1999. Available from 1018 Water St., Suite 201, Port Townsend, WA 98368.
James Q. Wilson	"A Gap in the Curriculum," *The New York Times*, April 26, 1999.

For Further Discussion

Chapter 1

1. Kenneth Lloyd Billingsley and Bill Owens contend that youth violence is a serious problem, while Mike Males asserts that adults, not teenagers, are responsible for most violent crimes. Whose view or views do you find most convincing and why?

2. Matthew Gore and Michael A. Males argue that the media exaggerate the crime rate and make violence seem more prevalent than it actually is. Do you think that the media, in particular television and newspapers, provide an inaccurate depiction of violence in society? Explain your answer.

3. Erica Goode and Patricia Pearson provide a variety of statistics to bolster their respective arguments on the problem of domestic violence. Do you find one author's statistics more compelling than the other's? In particular, what statistic do you find more convincing—that only four percent of women in violent relationships are severely injured, according to Pearson, or Goode's claim that approximately one-third of female homicide victims are killed by a former or current partner? Explain your answers.

Chapter 2

1. The authors in this chapter present a variety of theories as to why some people are violent. Which theories, if any, do you find most plausible? What other causes for violence would you suggest? Explain your answers, drawing from any relevant readings or experiences.

2. Bettyann H. Kevles and Daniel J. Kevles argue that earlier theories that linked biology to violence were often racist. They also express concern that current theories might lead to the stigmatizing of individuals whose brain scans suggest a propensity toward violence. Do you agree with their worries, and do you think that any stigmatism, if it occurs, will be racist? Why or why not?

3. Richard J. Gelles lists a variety of factors for male violence against women. What factor, if any, do you find most compelling and why?

Chapter 3

1. Elizabeth K. Carll is a psychologist whose specialties include understanding the causes of family violence, while Jack Valenti is the president of the Motion Picture Association of America. Based on their career backgrounds, who do you think is better

able to explain the effects of media violence and why? Explain your answer.

2. James Garbarino contends that boys who grow up with abusive fathers are more likely to turn to violence, while Don Feder maintains that corporal punishment is a necessary form of discipline that will help prevent youth violence. Do you think that parents should be stricter with their children or do you believe that physical punishment can increase the likelihood that the child will turn to violence? Explain your answer.

3. Do you agree with Robert Tracinski's conclusion that selfish goals are the only way to counter the nihilism that appeals to young men such as Eric Harris and Dylan Klebold? Why or why not?

Chapter 4

1. Do you agree with the premise, stated by Edmund F. McGarrell, that gun possession can in fact reduce violent crime? Why or why not?

2. After reading the viewpoints by Vincent L. Ferrandino and Gerald N. Tirozzi, and Richard L. Curwin and Allen N. Mendler, do you think zero-tolerance policies can be effective? Why or why not?

3. After reading the viewpoints in this chapter, what other solutions do you think can be effective in reducing violence? Explain your answers.

Organizations to Contact

The editors have compiled the following list of organizations concerned with issues debated in this book. The descriptions are derived from materials provided by the organizations. All have publications or information available for interested readers. The list was compiled on the date of publication of the present volume; the information provided here may change. Be aware that many organizations take several weeks or longer to respond to inquiries, so allow as much time as possible.

Coalition to Stop Gun Violence (CSGV)

1000 16th St. NW, Suite 603, Washington, DC 20002
(202) 530-0340 • fax: (202) 530-0331
e-mail: noguns@aol.com • website: www.gunfree.org

Formerly the National Coalition to Ban Handguns, CSGV lobbies at the local, state, and federal levels to ban the sale of handguns and assault weapons to individuals. It also litigates cases against firearms makers. Its publications include various informational sheets on gun violence and the paper "The Unspoken Tragedy: Firearm Suicide in the United States."

Crime Control Policy Center

Herman Kahn Center, 5395 Emerson Way, Indianapolis, IN 46226
(317) 545-1000 • fax: (317) 545-9639
website: www.hudson.org/crime2/index.html

The Crime Control Policy Center, operated under the auspices of the public policy research organization Hudson Institute, studies crime and justice issues in order to identify effective strategies for reducing crime and building safe neighborhoods and communities. Strategies the center has studied include restorative justice practices and reducing illegal drug use. Publications include articles in the Hudson Institute's magazine, *American Outlook*, and books such as *Targeting Firearms Crime Through Directed Police Patrol*.

Discipline Associates

PO Box 20481, Rochester, NY 14602
website: www.disciplineassociates.com

Founded by Dr. Richard Curwin and Dr. Allen Mendler, Discipline Associates provides training programs to help educators and administrators manage behavior and improve student responsibility. Books include *As Tough as Necessary: Countering Violence, Aggression, and Hostility in Our Schools* and *Discipline with Dignity*.

Gang and Youth Crime Prevention Program (GYCPP)
Ministry of Attorney General, Community Justice Branch
207-815 Hornby St., Vancouver, BC V6Z 2E6 Canada
(604) 660-2605 • hotline: (800) 680-4264 (British Columbia only)
fax: (604) 775-2674

This program works with government ministries, police, public agencies, community-based organizations, and youth in order to raise awareness, and reduce the incidence, of gang- and youth-related crime and violence. GYCPP maintains a youth violence directory, conducts forums and workshops, creates videos, and publishes a set of booklets on Canada's criminal justice system.

Handgun Control
1225 Eye St. NW, Suite 1100, Washington, DC 20005
(202) 898-0792 • fax: (202) 371-9615
website: www.handguncontrol.org

Handgun Control is an organization that does not want to ban guns but instead campaigns for gun safety legislation. Its publications include the issue briefs "Kids and Guns" and "Preventing Crime and Prosecuting Criminals."

Milton S. Eisenhower Foundation
1660 L St. NW, Suite 200, Washington, DC 20036
(202) 429-0440
website: www.eisenhowerfoundation.org

The foundation consists of individuals dedicated to reducing crime in inner-city neighborhoods through community programs. It believes that more federally funded programs such as Head Start and Job Corps would improve education and job opportunities for youths, thus reducing juvenile crime and violence. The foundation's publications include the report "Youth Investment and Police Mentoring" and the monthly newsletter *Challenges from Within*.

National Coalition Against Domestic Violence (NCADV)
PO Box 18749, Denver, CO 80218-0749
(303) 839-1852 • fax: (303) 831-9251
website: www.ncadv.org

NCADV serves as a national information and referral network on domestic violence issues. Its publications include *Every Home a Safe Home*, *Teen Dating Violence Resource Manual* and the quarterly newsletter *NCADV Update*.

National Crime Prevention Council (NCPC)
1000 Connecticut Ave. NW, 13th Floor, Washington, DC 20036
(202) 466-6272 • fax: (202)296-1356

NCPC provides training and technical assistance to groups and individuals interested in crime prevention. It advocates job training and recreation programs as means to reduce youth crime and violence. The council, which sponsors the Take a Bite Out of Crime campaign, publishes the books *Preventing Violence: Program Ideas and Examples* and *350 Tested Strategies to Prevent Crime*, the booklet "Making Children, Families, and Communities Safer From Violence," and the newsletter *Catalyst*.

National Rifle Association (NRA)
11250 Waples Mill Rd., Fairfax, VA 22030
(703) 267-1160 • fax: (703) 267-3992
website: www.nra.org

The key goals of the NRA are defending American's Second Amendment rights and teaching Americans how to use guns safely. The organization lobbies against legislation, such as gun licensing and registration, that restricts the ability of law-abiding citizens to own and purchase guns. The NRA publishes the magazines *American Rifleman*, *American Hunter*, and *America's 1st Freedom*.

National Institute of Justice (NIJ)
810 Seventh St. NW, Washington, DC 20531
(202) 307-2942 • fax: (202) 307-6394
website: www.ojp.usdoj.gov/nij

NIJ is the primary federal sponsor of research on crime and its control. It sponsors research efforts through grants and contracts that are carried out by universities, private institutions, and state and local agencies. Its publications include "Comparing the Criminal Behavior of Youth Gangs and At-Risk Youths" and "High School Youths, Weapons, and Violence: A National Survey."

National School Safety Center (NSSC)
141 Duesenberg Dr., Suite 11, Westlake Village, CA 91362
(805) 373-9977 • fax: (805) 373-9277
e-mail: info@nssc1.org • website: www.nssc1.org

Part of Pepperdine University, the center is a research organization that studies school crime and violence, including gang and hate crimes, and provides technical assistance to local school systems. NSSC believes that teacher training is an effective way of reducing juvenile crime. It publishes the *School Safety Update* newsletter, published nine times a year, and the resource papers "Safe Schools Overview" and "Weapons in Schools."

Bibliography of Books

Gil Bailie	*Violence Unveiled: Humanity at the Crossroads.* New York: Crossroad, 1995.
Joel Best	*Random Violence: How We Talk About New Crimes and New Victims.* Berkeley: University of California Press, 1999.
Sissela Bok	*Mayhem: Violence as Public Entertainment.* Reading, MA: Addison-Wesley, 1998.
Carl Bosch	*Schools Under Siege: Guns, Gangs, and Hidden Dangers.* Springfield, NJ: Enslow, 1997.
Nona H. Cannon	*Roots of Violence, Seeds of Peace in People, Families, and Society.* San Diego: Miclearoy, 1996.
Elizabeth K. Carll, ed.	*Violence in Our Lives: Impact on Workplace, Home, and Community.* Boston: Allyn and Bacon, 1999.
Philip W. Cook	*Abused Men: The Hidden Side of Domestic Violence* Westport, CT: Praeger, 1997.
Rene Denfeld	*Kill the Body, the Head Will Fall: A Closer Look at Women, Violence, and Aggression.* New York: Warner, 1997.
John Devine	*Maximum Security: The Culture of Violence in Inner-City Schools.* Chicago: University of Chicago Press, 1996.
Peter T. Elikann	*Superpredators: The Demonization of Our Children by the Law.* Reading, MA: Perseus, 1999.
Peter T. Elikann	*The Tough-on-Crime Myth: Real Solutions to Cut Crime.* New York: Insight, 1996.
Raymond B. Flannery Jr.	*Violence in America: Coping with Drugs, Distressed Families, Inadequate Schooling, and Acts of Hate.* New York: Continuum, 1997.
Patricia Riddle Gaddis	*Dangerous Dating: Helping Young Women Say No to Abusive Relationships.* Wheaton, IL: Harold Shaw, 2000.
James Garbarino	*Lost Boys: Why Our Sons Turn Violent and How We Can Save Them.* New York: Free, 1999.
James Gilligan	*Violence: Our Deadly Epidemic and Its Causes.* New York: G.P. Putnam, 1996.
Dave Grossman and Gloria DeGaetano	*Stop Teaching Our Kids to Kill: A Call to Action Against TV, Movie, and Video Game Violence.* New York: Crown, 1999.
Michele Harway and James M. O'Neil, eds.	*What Causes Men's Violence Against Women?* Thousand Oaks, CA: Sage, 1999.

Arturo Hernandez	*Peace in the Streets: Breaking the Cycle of Gang Violence*. Washington, DC: Child Welfare League of America, 1998.
James C. Howell	*Juvenile Justice and Youth Violence*. Thousand Oaks, CA: Sage, 1997.
Valerie Jenness and Kendal Broad	*Hate Crimes: New Social Movements and the Politics of Violence* New York: Aldine de Gruyter, 1997.
Robin Karr-Morse and Meredith S. Wiley	*Ghosts from the Nursery: Tracing the Roots of Violence*. New York: Atlantic Monthly, 1997.
Michael D. Kelleher	*New Arenas for Violence: Homicide in the American Workplace*. Westport, CT: Praeger, 1996.
Bob Larson	*Extreme Evil: Kids Killing Kids*. Nashville: T. Nelson, 1999.
Beth Leventhal and Sandra E. Lundy, eds.	*Same-Sex Domestic Violence: Strategies for Change*. Thousand Oaks, CA: Sage, 1999.
Mike A. Males	*Framing Youth: Ten Myths About the Next Generation*. Monroe, ME: Common Courage, 1998.
Mike A. Males	*The Scapegoat Generation: America's War on Adolescents*. Monroe, ME: Common Courage, 1996.
Joseph Marshall Jr. and Lonnie Wheeler	*Street Soldier: One Man's Struggle to Save a Generation—One Life at a Time*. New York: Bantam Doubleday Dell, 1996.
Joan McCord, ed.	*Violence and Childhood in the Inner City*. Cambridge, UK: Cambridge University Press, 1997.
Michael Medved and Diane Medved	*Saving Childhood: Protecting Our Children from the National Assault on Innocence*. New York: HarperCollins/Zondervan, 1998.
Patricia Pearson	*When She Was Bad: Violent Women and the Myth of Innocence*. New York: Viking, 1997.
Public Agenda	*Violent Kids: Can We Change the Trend?* Dubuque, IA: Kendall/Hunt, 2000.
Richard Rhodes	*Why They Kill: The Discoveries of a Maverick Criminologist*. New York: Alfred A. Knopf, 1999.
Ved Varma, ed.	*Violence in Children and Adolescents* London: Jessica Kingsley, 1997.
Elaine Weiss	*Surviving Domestic Violence: Voices of Women Who Broke Free*. Salt Lake City: Agreka, 2000.
Richard Wrangham and Dale Peterson	*Demonic Males: Apes and the Origins of Human Violence*. Boston: Houghton Mifflin, 1996.
Franklin E. Zimring	*American Youth Violence*. New York: Oxford University Press, 1998.

Index

192